Benazir Bhutto

ALSO BY BROOKE ALLEN

Twentieth-Century Attitudes: Literary Powers in Uncertain Times

Artistic License: Three Centuries of Good Writing and Bad Behavior

Moral Minority: Our Skeptical Founding Fathers

The Other Side of the Mirror: An American Travels Through Syria

Forthcoming, with Nile Southern:
Yours in Haste and Adoration: The Selected Letters of Terry Southern

Benazir Bhutto

FAVORED DAUGHTER

BROOKE ALLEN

ICONS SERIES

New Harvest
Houghton Mifflin Harcourt
BOSTON . NEW YORK
2016

Library of Congress Cataloging-in-Publication Data
Allen, Brooke, author.
Benazir Bhutto : favored daughter / Brooke Allen.
pages ; cm. — (Icons series)
ISBN 978-0-544-64893-7 (hardcover)
1. Bhutto, Benazir, 1953–2007. 2. Women prime ministers —
Pakistan — Biography. 3. Pakistan — Politics and government.
I. Title. II. Series: Icons series (New Harvest (Firm))
DS389.22.B48A53 2015
954.9105'2092 — dc23
[B]
2015015215

Printed in the United States of America
DOC 10 9 8 7 6 5 4 3 2 1

To the White family: Lucy, John Michael, Amy.
With infinite thanks for the many happy hours on
their front porch — the Great Good Place.

Contents

Introduction

W HEN THE BEAUTIFUL and courageous Benazir Bhutto became prime minister of Pakistan in 1988, after the country had undergone eleven years of military dictatorship, she became an international symbol of youth, hope, and democracy. Less than a decade later, with her two terms at the helm of government blighted by inaction, lack of direction, and a level of corruption that in the end could only be described as kleptocracy, she had proved a major disappointment for the Pakistani people.

Yet for many Westerners, the glorious image has never quite been tarnished. She still seems to be, despite her manifest failures, everything we think we want in a Muslim leader. As the South Asian expert William Dalrymple has written, "For the Americans, what Benazir Bhutto wasn't was possibly more attractive even than what she was. She wasn't a religious fundamentalist, she didn't have a beard, she didn't organize rallies where everyone shouts: 'Death to America' and she didn't issue fatwas against Booker-winning authors."[1] Neither, it should be added, was she a mustachioed army general, a refreshing change in its own right. And perhaps most significantly, she wasn't a socialist, like her father, Zulfikar Ali Bhutto, the democratically elected prime minister whose judicial murder in 1979 after a military coup had gone unlamented in Washington's corridors of power. During his years in authority Z. A. Bhutto had distanced Pakistan from the United States by removing it from the American-led Southeast Asia Treaty Organization and pursuing a policy of nominal nonalignment, while in practice cozying up to Mao's China. Benazir, by delightful contrast, was a thorough neoliberal and far from anti-American; she even became chums with the Iron Lady herself, Margaret Thatcher, whose strong-arm methods she admired and eventually emulated.

Benazir Bhutto entitled her autobiography *Daughter of the East,* but she might just as easily be called a daughter of the West. Or, more precisely, a product of the uneasy, mutually suspicious, and mutually exploitative relationship that has existed between East and West, between the Muslim world, particularly Pakistan, and the United States since the latter assumed the imperial role abandoned by the British after World War II. Educated, as her father had been, both in England and America, Benazir appeared to be "one of us": she acquired a Western veneer that manifested itself, at the baseline level, in a taste for peppermint-stick ice cream and pop psychology, and on a higher plane in a steeping in and apparent respect for democratic government — whether of the parliamentary or the presidential variety — based on Enlightenment principles of legal equality and the consent of the governed. She had served, after all, as president of the Oxford Union, the nursery of great British politicians like Gladstone and Macmillan, Wilson and Heath; before that, at Harvard's Radcliffe College during the Vietnam era, she had soaked up the impassioned rhetoric of the antiwar and women's liberation movements that were revolutionizing American culture. So when she entered the political arena upon the arrest and subsequent execution of her father, it seemed she might bring a style of Western democracy to the apparently endless Pakistani cycle of civilian rule followed by military takeover — a process her father, Z. A. Bhutto, had dubbed "coup-gemony." And then there was the fact that she was a woman: as the press perpetually reminded us, she was the first woman to be elected leader of a

Muslim nation. (Pakistan's population is 97 percent Muslim, a substantial percentage of which is religiously and socially conservative.)

It was indeed a remarkable achievement for a Radcliffe peacenik to rise to become the leader of conservative Pakistan. And yet as a look at the history of that nation's geographical neighbors indicates, Benazir Bhutto's electoral victory in 1988 was not so much a sign of the unprecedented relaxation of Pakistani religious prejudice as it was a reminder that Pakistan was historically a part of India and remains Indian in many features, including the acceptance of female leadership if the woman in question happens to be carrying on the mission of a husband or father. Since the breakup of British India in 1947, there have been several such examples: Indira Gandhi picking up the torch from her father, Jawaharlal Nehru, India's first prime minister; Sirimavo Bandaranaike of Sri Lanka, who took office as prime minister in 1960 after the assassination of her husband; Ms. Bhutto herself, avenging her charismatic father; and Khaleda Zia, widow of the Bangladeshi leader Ziaur Rahman, who in 1991 led their party to victory in the national elections of this other Muslim country. (Five years later another woman, a daughter of Bangladeshi founding father Mujibur Rahman, would head that government.) And then there was the redoubtable Fatima Jinnah, sister of the Pakistani founding father Muhammad Ali Jinnah, who at the age of seventy-two challenged the military dictator Ayub Khan in a presidential race. If anything, female leadership has become a regular subcontinental tradition, with Ian Buruma going so far as to posit that the importance in Hinduism of the "Great Mother, who can be both horribly destructive and divinely benevolent," has had a strong influence on subcontinental politics in both Hindu and Muslim nations.[2] That's a possibility, but what is certain is that the dynastic principle holds, democracy or no democracy.

And this is perhaps particularly true in Pakistan, where the feudal system was never broken after the departure of the British. In India, Nehru's socialist policies and reforms, enacted over his seventeen-year leadership, did dislodge many of the old power structures, but this was not the case in Pakistan, where the hold of the "feudals," and in particular the famous "twenty-two families" who in 1968 were said to control two-thirds of the nation's industrial assets, still has not loosened today, nearly seven decades after independence. And the Bhuttos were — and still are — among the most powerful of Pakistan's great feudal families. They are aristocrats, and they are fully aware of that fact: Benazir behaved throughout her career as though she had been born to rule by divine right, and her brother Murtaza apparently felt the same, though he was to meet with less political success. As the years went on, the giggly girl who had been so popular with her Oxford and Harvard cohort disappeared, while the imperious woman who brooked no opposition inside or outside of her party gradually took her place. "The insolent look with which she squares up to the microphone," Christopher Hitchens wrote of Bhutto, "turns her profile with each alternate sentence, and, in the old-fashioned sense, *addresses* the crowd, is a look that money can't buy... It is the legacy of breeding, in a country conditioned by generations of colonial rule and feudalism."[3] Of course Western democracies have also had aristocrats as leaders over the course of the twentieth century — Winston Churchill, grandson of a duke, and Franklin Roosevelt, scion of one of America's great families, are only the most obvious, and the first to spring to mind — but they never, as both Zulfikar and Benazir Bhutto did, treated their political parties as personal demesnes to which they were entitled by birth.

The Bhuttos have often been likened to the Kennedys, and it is true that for sheer drama — tragedy, wealth, beauty, violent death, corruption, treachery — it would be hard to choose between the two families. And like several members of the

Kennedy family, Benazir had outsize flaws to match her outsize gifts. But it might be even more telling to go back further and look at the House of Atreus, to whose violent history that of the Bhuttos might easily be compared. Or, to go down a peg, to multigenerational soap operas like *Dynasty* or *Dallas*. For one thing is true: as Benazir's Harvard friend the journalist Amy Wilentz has pointed out, Benazir Bhutto led "a veritable *telenovela* of a life."[4]

I

IT IS IMPOSSIBLE to get a grip on Benazir Bhutto and her tremendous sense of personal destiny without some understanding of the anachronistic milieu of which she was a product: feudal, rural Pakistan. The Bhutto clan's ancestors were Hindu Rajputs from Rajasthan, who according to family lore converted to Islam after the Muslim invasion of India in the eighth century. The patriarch from whom Benazir's branch of the family would descend, Sheto, rose to a position of power under the Mughal emperor Aurangzeb in the seventeenth century, claiming the title of khan, or clan leader. As one historian of the family has put it, "as far back as history traces them, Bhuttos have been adroit at seizing whatever opportunities life offered, equally ready to move on or change their faith if they deemed it expedient for survival's sake."[1] Sheto Khan moved to Sindh, in the southernmost province of what would in 1947 become Pakistan, settling near the town of Larkana, which remains the Bhutto power base to this day.

It is an immemorial landscape: thousands of acres of arid salt flats. Larkana is near the site of Mohenjo Daro in the Indus Valley, one of the world's earliest urban settlements. The proximity to this cradle of civilization has seemed significant to the Bhuttos, as Benazir recounted in her autobiography: "As a small child I thought the ancient city was called 'Munj Jo Dero,' which in Sindhi means 'my place.' My brothers, sister and I took great pride that we had been raised in the shadow of Moenjo-daro, that we lived on the bank of the Indus which had been bringing life to the land since the beginnings of time."[2]

The British conquest of Sindh, carried out in 1842–3 by Sir Charles Napier, was a brutal affair in which some ten thousand native Sindhis perished. The Bhuttos, however, were loyal to the British and were rewarded accordingly, with Napier singling out the head of the family, at that time Dodo Khan Bhutto, for special favors. Dodo Khan consolidated the immense family holdings in Sindh, while Bhuttos from other branches of this large extended family received titles from the queen-empress and land from the Raj administration. At the height of the family's power, Bhutto land in Sindh stretched nearly eighty miles — a demesne that dwarfed comparable aristocratic hold-ings in Europe.

Benazir and her siblings were encouraged to take the ro-mantic view of their family's history, to see the Bhuttos not as loyal, well-compensated servants of their British overlords but as freebooting mavericks. A favorite family story was that of Benazir's great-grandfather Mir Ghulam Murtaza Bhutto, who had attracted the affections of a British woman — a love that was of course unthinkable under the nineteenth-century Raj. The Bhutto version of the tale had Ghulam Murtaza defiantly horse-whipping the British colonel who had warned him off his mem-sahib, taking refuge with the royal family of Afghanistan, and finally returning to Sindh only to be poisoned by his nefari-ous enemies. The research of Z. A. Bhutto's biographer, Stanley Wolpert, has unearthed a less colorful and romantic version of this story; still, Ghulam Murtaza's place in the family mythol-ogy is significant. Bhuttos were to be depicted not as servants of the Raj but as swashbuckling cavaliers. The glowing pride dis-played by both Benazir and her father in the more extravagant ways of their feudal forebears was always glaringly at odds with their stated populism; it is one of the central paradoxes of their careers.

The Indian Congress Party was founded in 1885, and from that time nationalists applied pressure on the British for independence. This pressure was to increase sharply after World War I, when Britain reneged on promises to move toward Indian independence even though India, in good faith, had sent more than a million men to fight for the British. Between the wars a measure of self-government began to be accorded the subjects of the Raj, though the authorities attempted to control the subcontinent by recruiting the hereditary landowners (known as *zamindars* or *waderos*) into the civil service, the police, and the political arena, rewarding them for loyalty and cooperation. In 1926 the first elections for the new Central Legislative Assembly were conducted in Sindh; seat 207 was contested and won by Sardar Wahid Baksh Bhutto. From that time through independence, the creation of Pakistan, and beyond, seat 207 would belong to the Bhuttos, an indication of the tight hold on power that feudal landlords have maintained right into the twenty-first century. This was the seat from which the young Zulfikar Ali Bhutto would launch himself into power. The Bhuttos were never in much danger of losing it, for in feudal Pakistan the largely illiterate masses have voted as their tribal leaders dictate: in 1988, when Zulfikar's widow Nusrat ran for the Larkana seat in the National Assembly, she polled 97 percent of the vote — and no one was surprised.

The tempestuous and colorful Ghulam Murtaza had a son, Shah Nawaz, who would work closely with the British as the Indian subcontinent moved slowly and painfully toward independence. In 1920 Shah Nawaz won the one seat allotted to Sindh on the Imperial Legislative Council at Delhi, and began presiding over the District Board and Central Co-Operative Bank of Larkana; he also became the president of the Sindh Mohammedan Association and, eventually, of the Sindh United

Party. In 1930 he was named one of sixteen Muslim delegates from all of British India to attend the first of three Imperial Round Table conferences in London, where he was able to convince India's rulers that Sindh should be awarded separate provincial status; this was an important move, for it legally elevated Sindh's capital, Karachi, from its position as a relatively obscure port town to a capital city on an equal footing with the great metropolises of Calcutta, Madras, and Bombay. In 1934, he cofounded the Sindh People's Party. He enjoyed a close working relationship with the British and became the leading Muslim confidant to the governor at Bombay, Lord Brabourne. India's rulers in Whitehall rewarded Shah Nawaz by making him a Companion of the Order of the British Empire and, later, bestowing upon him a knighthood.

In 1946 Sir Shah Nawaz Bhutto rose to become the prime minister of Junagadh, one of India's 565 so-called princely states, which were nominally independent so long as they cooperated with British interests. It was a key moment in subcontinental history. As independence and partition of the country into the new states of India and Pakistan approached, slated for mid-1947, the problem of what to do with the princely states became pressing. The ultimate decision was that each prince should decide which country his state would adhere to; Sir Shah Nawaz was instrumental in persuading his employer, the nawab of Junagadh, to opt for Pakistan. As the countdown to independence proceeded — August 14 for Pakistan, the next day for India — and the borders of the new countries were hastily drawn up by Sir Cyril Radcliffe, a British civil servant who had no previous knowledge of the subcontinent and was armed with out-of-date and inadequate maps, panic and chaos ensued. The tragic story of the partition, during which twelve and a half million people were displaced and at least a million, perhaps many more, killed in ethnic violence by both Hindus and Muslims, is well known. Things went no more smoothly in Junagadh than elsewhere: when the time came, Indian troops seized the state and the nawab fled into exile.

Sir Shah Nawaz's grand plan had failed, but his career was nonetheless impressive. As Zulfikar Ali Bhutto's biographer, Stanley Wolpert, wrote, "No opportunity for early political advancement eluded Shah Nawaz. He was careful to seize any advantage for his family's fast-rising fortune, and never forgot his loyalty, almost as great as that premier loyalty to the Bhutto family, to his region and its people."[3] He made a powerful mentor for his brilliant and ambitious son, and, indirectly, for his granddaughter Benazir.

For all his Anglicization, Sir Shah Nawaz maintained a traditional Muslim family life. The custom among the great Muslim *wadero* clans was for sons and daughters to marry cousins so as to keep land and property in the family. Up to four wives per husband was acceptable in theory, though not always approved of in practice, and wives were kept in purdah in family quarters at the family's central household. Shah Nawaz's first wife was, as prescribed by tradition, a cousin. Their elder son died of tuberculosis at the age of seven; the second, Imdad Ali, his father's heir apparent, grew into a handsome playboy and a heavy drinker.

These senior, inconvenient male Bhuttos are not acknowledged in Benazir's autobiography. The formative influence on her life in every way was her father, Zulfikar Ali Bhutto, the Agamemnon to her Electra. As far as she was concerned, Shah Nawaz's family began with his second marriage — a love match — to a teenage Hindu dancing girl, Lakhi Bai. Lakhi Bai converted to Islam in order to marry Shah Nawaz in 1925, changing her name to Khurshid, and joined her husband's first wife in purdah at Larkana, where she gave birth to two daughters and then, in 1928, to Zulfikar Ali.

Zulfi Bhutto would spend much of his childhood in Bombay, where his father was summoned in 1934 to join the cabinet of the colonial governor, Lord Brabourne. The boy was enrolled in Bombay's prestigious Cathedral High School at the early age of nine. Four years later he, like his father before him, was required by his parents to contract a feudal marriage to a Bhutto cousin. Shireen was eight or nine years older than the thirteen-year-old Zulfi; upon marriage she assumed the name of Amir Begum, and like the other Bhutto women, she settled quietly into the purdah quarters at Larkana. As a result of this union Zulfi would inherit one-third of his father-in-law's estate upon the latter's death, land still in the possession of the Bhutto family today.

Benazir, a product of her father's second, "love" marriage, clearly found it awkward to reveal these facts to the Western world, again taking the apparent line in her autobiography that the less said about this unfortunate marriage, a stain on the Bhuttos' carefully cultivated image as modern, reform-minded Muslims, the better. And a certain amount of mystery still hovers around the relationship, if in fact there was one to speak of, between Z. A. Bhutto and Amir Begum. He would claim to his second wife that the marriage had been enacted purely to secure the property, and that there had never been any physical contact between the couple. After the ceremony, the adolescent bridegroom did indeed return to his school and his cricket matches. But some of Zulfikar's friends have claimed that he enjoyed the occasional sexual encounter with his first bride over the years, and even that Amir Begum gave birth to a daughter. But this claim remains unsubstantiated. The fact that no one seems to know for sure is a sign of the isolation in which the women of feudal families like the Bhuttos lived, effectively cut off from the outside world.

In the meantime, Zulfi went on with his schooling. Sir Shah Nawaz had not finished secondary school: most feudal families of his era had seen no need for their sons, who would be large-scale landowners, to waste their time on education. But Shah

Nawaz felt that his lack of education had put him at a disadvantage in his dealings with both the British and the Hindus, and he was determined to send his sons to a university, preferably abroad. Zulfi was undeniably brilliant, but careless and mercurial. He failed his entrance examination to Cambridge, and his father decided he should attend an American school for a while before his next attempt at an Oxbridge college. He was also rejected by Harvard and UC Berkeley, but accepted at the University of Southern California, in Los Angeles.

One of the reasons these early academic results were not commensurate with Zulfi's obvious intelligence was that he had already been bitten by the political bug — and how could he not have been, considering the times? He was completing his secondary education during the last years of World War II, during which time the "Quit India" campaign reached a crescendo and Indian political leaders and agitators were in and out of British prisons. It was becoming clear that the British would indeed quit India sometime after the war, and sooner rather than later. The question of Pakistan — whether it would come into being at all, what kind of a state it would be, what sort of a constitution it might have — was urgent. Zulfi Bhutto, a political insider due to his father's influence, was one of a select group of Muslim students invited to discuss direct political action with Muhammad Ali Jinnah, the Bombay lawyer who led the All-India Muslim League and would become the first governor-general of independent Pakistan, the country's founding father and *Qaid-i-Azam* (Great Leader). The young Bhutto was an ardent advocate of a Muslim state. "Musalmans," he wrote Jinnah at the tender age of seventeen, "should realize that the Hindus can never and will never unite with us, they are the deadliest enemies of our Koran and our Prophet . . . Being still in school I am unable to help the establishment of our sacred land. But the time will come when I will even sacrifice my life for Pakistan."[4] It was a grimly prescient remark.

Z. A. Bhutto's years of study in the United States would begin a lifelong love-hate relationship with all things American. As a brown-skinned man, he had to submit to the color bar and the Jim Crow laws — though as a subject of the Raj he would hardly have been unfamiliar with racial prejudice and segregation. He also felt a powerful resistance to the Cold War ideology that swept the country during his years in the United States, and that would soon grip newly independent Pakistan in an American stranglehold: as president (and later prime minister), Bhutto would spend his years in power leading Pakistan away from the American alliance and realigning his country toward China and the communist world. During his four years in California he was active not only in campus politics but also in the national arena, enthusiastically volunteering in the liberal Helen Gahagan Douglas's unsuccessful 1950 Senate bid against Richard Nixon. But in spite of Zulfikar's disaffection from the American political mainstream, he would eventually send his three older children to Harvard for their own exposure to the American establishment; he considered an American education, and powerful American connections, to be an indispensable component of their political and diplomatic formation.

After two years at USC Bhutto transferred to Berkeley, from which he graduated with a degree in political science in 1950. Now he was ready for Oxford, where he studied jurisprudence and law at Christ Church College, completing his studies in two years rather than the recommended three. He then moved on to London, where in 1953 he was called to the bar at Lincoln's Inn.

Two years previously he had married the lovely Nusrat Ispahani. Amir Begum was of course still tucked away at Larkana; Nusrat would turn out to be Zulfi's *official* wife, the kind of modern, Westernized, left-liberal consort Z. A. Bhutto required. She was a natural for the job, every bit as attractive as he was. A year younger than her husband, she had been born in

Bombay to Kurdish Iranian parents; her father was a businessman who moved his family to Karachi after partition and set
himself up as a soap manufacturer. As she was a member of the
urban bourgeoisie, her expectations from life were very different from those of the feudal Bhuttos. She had participated in
the larger world, even reaching the rank of captain in the Pakistan Women's National Guard.

Needless to say, Zulfi's family resisted this love match; busi-
nessmen's daughters were not good enough for the aristocratic
Bhuttos. On top of that, Nusrat was a Shi'ite. Zulfi reminded
his father that he himself had married a Hindu, and from a social class considerably below that of Nusrat. Undeterred by pa-
rental resistance, he married her on September 8, 1951.

She immediately proved herself a political asset. They made
a striking pair, she with her classical beauty and elegance, he
with the beginnings of the charisma for which he would soon
become legendary. His energy, charm, and overweening self-
confidence were heightened by an artist's attention to personal
style. There is a British Commonwealth counterpart to the
American limousine liberal that might well be called the Savile Row socialist, and Zulfikar, like his mentor Muhammad Ali
Jinnah before him, was one of its prototypes. With his bespoke
suits, Turnbull & Asser shirts, Cuban cigars, Scotch whiskey,
and the inevitable whiff of Shalimar cologne, Z. A. Bhutto indicated his wealth, his good taste, and a certain reckless glamour. In later years he would don a Mao cap at political rallies,
but this was a mere prop: the Savile Row persona was the one he
reveled in, the one that came the closest to projecting the "real"
man.

In her autobiography Benazir claimed that after her parents' marriage, Nusrat entered purdah for a time with the other
Bhutto women. But this appears to have been a fabrication. In
actuality, according to Wolpert's careful research, the newly-
weds proceeded just days after their Karachi wedding to Istan-

bul, Rome, and then London, where they stayed in a suite at the Dorchester and enjoyed a performance of *South Pacific*. They then shuttled between Oxford and London while Zulfi completed his studies and began his legal apprenticeship. It was not until Nusrat was ready to become a mother that she returned to Karachi, while her husband stayed in London.

Why might Benazir have come up with the story that her mother entered purdah? Her 1988 autobiography (augmented in 2007, shortly before her death) is preeminently a political performance, written — at the very moment of her rise to power — for a Western readership, with the clear agenda of seducing Western opinion and opinion-makers. (In England it was entitled *Daughter of the East,* in America *Daughter of Destiny;* the subtle reasoning behind the differentiation of the two audiences is a political choice in its own right.) One of the images Benazir was trying to project was that of the groundbreaker, the shatterer of ancient prejudices and outmoded traditions: a liberated, enlightened woman. If her mother was revealed as having been liberated and enlightened a generation earlier than she was, it would detract considerably from Benazir's own status as the great breaker of gender barriers.

Another dubious claim of Benazir's is that her mother initially made her wear a burqa when she reached adolescence. According to Benazir's account, Nusrat told her — albeit with reluctance — that she was no longer a child, and produced the burqa from her bag and draped it over her; later that evening, her father ruled that she did not need to wear it. Again, this story rings false. Why would Nusrat, who did not wear the burqa herself, decide that her daughter should do so? Again, was Benazir simply trying to present herself as a first — in this case, the first Bhutto woman to escape the veil?

In any event, there is no evidence that Nusrat entered purdah. She was living in Karachi when Benazir, immediately nicknamed Pinkie due to her rosy color, arrived on June 21, 1953.

(Anglicized pet names like Pinkie are not uncommon among the daughters of Pakistan's ruling class: the heroine of Moni Mohsin's 2008 satirical novel, *Diary of a Social Butterfly,* has girlfriends with monikers like Flopsy, Furry, and Twinkle — not to mention an Aunty Pussy.)

At the time of his elder child's birth, Zulfikar was still in England. He would not meet her until six months later.

2

YEARS LATER, Benazir Bhutto claimed that her father had named her his political heir, but there is no evidence whatever for this assertion aside from her own word for it, and others in her family, including her mother, Nusrat, have hotly denied it. And indeed it would have been an eccentric choice for the father of two sons in an overwhelmingly patriarchal society. What *is* true is that there appears to have been a special bond between father and daughter. The two had much in common: strength, charisma, political instinct, and the courage, part and parcel of their arrogance, that was so characteristic of both.

Benazir (the name means "without flaw") was soon followed by three siblings: Mir Murtaza in 1954, Sanam in 1957, and Shah Nawaz in 1958. Their father was moving quickly up the ladder, both politically and financially. One dramatic change to his status came when his playboy half brother, Imdad Ali, died of cirrhosis of the liver in 1953, so that when Sir Shah Nawaz in turn died in 1957, Zulfi inherited all of his immense landholdings, in addition to the lands Amir Begum had brought to him. He was now an extremely wealthy man. At this same period he was entering the political arena, writing opinion pieces, and inserting himself into the national discussion about the changes that were going on at the top of Pakistani politics.

Jinnah, the *Qaid-i-Azam*, had died in 1948, only a year after Pakistan came into existence. Three years later his successor, Liaquat Ali Khan, was assassinated in Rawalpindi. Many have blamed Pakistan's subsequent instability, its careering course between military and nominally democratic rule, on the fact that the new nation lost its founding father so quickly. In neighboring India, where Jawaharlal Nehru was prime minister from independence until his death in 1964 — a total of seventeen years — there was time for organic change to occur. But others have blamed Jinnah himself for the failure, and the Muslim League he led. Tariq Ali, one of the most clear-sighted commentators on Pakistani history and politics (and on the Bhutto family as well), has presented this case in rather brutal terms:

> Largely a stranger to the present provinces of West Pakistan, [Jinnah] simply confirmed the provincial landlords and feudalists in power as the representatives of his party there. The result was that the ruling elite in Pakistan never possessed a reliable political party capable of controlling the masses. The Muslim League soon became a clutch of corrupt and quarrelsome caciques who discredited it permanently. Pakistan was thus, from the outset, firmly dominated by its civilian bureaucracy and the army, both of which had faithfully served the British. The top echelon of each were composed of an exclusive English-educated elite ... In the first decade after partition, the civilian bureaucracy exercised political paramountcy in Pakistan. The CSP — Civil Service of Pakistan — comprised a closed oligarchy of five hundred functionaries commanding the state. Indeed, the two masterful heads of state of this period, Ghulam Mohammad (1951–5) and Iskander Mirza (1955–8), were co-opted directly from its ranks. They manipulated the token parliamentarianism of this time, until it became so discredited that in 1958 a military coup was engineered.[1]

This was the political background to Zulfikar's early career. As his father's son, he was extremely well connected; Sir Shah Nawaz had entertained Iskander Mirza, who succeeded Ghulam Mohammad as governor-general, at his legendary hunting parties in Larkana. Mirza took the young Zulfikar under his wing, urging him to join the Republican Party, which had just been founded with Mirza's blessing, and offering him the mayoralty of Karachi in 1957. Bhutto refused both these temptations: the Republicans, he believed, did not have enough popular support, and he did not want to get so bogged down in the hassle of administering a city that he lost touch with the bigger picture. From the very beginning he had set his sights on one day becoming foreign minister, and there can be no doubt, considering his perfectly open admiration for Napoleon, that he aspired eventually to become head of state. The decline of the Muslim League throughout the 1950s depressed him, though it would not be until a decade later that he would go on to cofound a new party.

In 1957 Zulfikar was part of the Pakistani delegation to the United Nations in New York, and the following year he chaired the Pakistani delegation at the UN Conference on the Law of the Sea at Geneva. He had been invited by Mirza to serve as minister of commerce when, in late 1958, the first of Pakistan's military coups occurred — in all likelihood with American backing, for elections were slated for early 1959 in which nationalist parties, if victorious, might have reneged on existing security pacts with the United States. The commander in chief of the army, Muhammed Ayub Khan, took power, assuming the title of president. Ayub, like most of the army's upper echelon during Pakistan's first decades, was highly Anglicized — according to Tariq Ali, a "jovial Sandhurst-trained officer, secular in outlook, fond of the odd drink, and used to obeying orders."[2] The orders, presumably, were now coming from Washington.

And indeed, Pakistan had been a key member of SEATO, the Southeast Asia Treaty Organization, since 1954.

Ayub decided to retain Mirza's newly sworn-in cabinet, so Zulfikar continued as minister of commerce, later acquiring several more portfolios: Information and Broadcasting, Village Aid, Basic Democracies, Tourism, Minorities. He became a firm bulwark of Ayub's regime, helping the military dictator to organize a referendum in 1960 that would give a mandate for his next five years in power and to draft the new constitution of 1962 that ended martial law. Ayub, though a military dictator, was a reformer and a secularist; he enacted Pakistan's first significant land reforms, removed the word "Islamic" from the official name of the republic, passed laws that made religious laws subservient to secular ones, promoted family planning, and discouraged the wearing of the burqa.

In the meantime, Benazir was taking the first steps on the educational path that her father had mapped out for her and her siblings. "In our house education was top priority," she wrote. "Like his father before him, my father wanted to make examples out of us, the next generation of educated and progressive Pakistanis."[3] She attended Lady Jennings Nursery School in Karachi, then the Convent of Jesus and Mary. Instruction at these institutions was in English, the same language the Bhuttos spoke at home — another example of upper-class Pakistani disconnection from the life of the masses. It seems astounding that the children of a socialist, populist politician grew up speaking only rudimentary Urdu and Sindhi, the languages of his constituents, and no Punjabi or Bengali, those of large swathes of the nation. But that was the way it was: the Bhuttos, like other great landowning families, were a breed apart.

Benazir presented the early years of the Bhutto family life as an idyll, but this was very far from being the case. Zulfikar was proprietary toward his wife but had no intention of curtailing the sex life he felt was his due as alpha male. His adventures were well known among his set in Karachi, and in 1961 he embarked on an affair with Husna Sheikh, the wife of a lawyer from East Pakistan. This time it was serious, and when Nusrat objected to the liaison Zulfikar was ruthless; he threw her out of the house.

This was not a situation Zulfikar's boss, Ayub Khan, was willing to tolerate, and he gave Bhutto an ultimatum: take Nusrat back or quit the cabinet. It was done, but with an ill grace, and rather than dropping the attractive Husna, Zulfikar simply set her up in a house in the posh neighborhood of Clifton, just a few minutes' walk from his own. Nusrat, distraught, decided to leave him, fleeing to her father's home in Iran. But Zulfikar refused to let his children out of the country. Nusrat lingered for six months in Iran, desolate without her children; in the end she gave in and returned, reluctantly, to Karachi. Eight years later she attempted suicide.

All these facts have been revealed by Stanley Wolpert in his biography of Zulfikar; before its 1993 publication they were unknown, and not many people outside of Pakistan know the story even now. Benazir steadfastly ignored not only her father's minor peccadilloes but this major one as well, and her writings make no mention of Husna Sheikh or indeed of any breach in the Bhutto family's flawless facade. Her decision to whitewash her family history so drastically must surely have been both personal and political. Politically, an admission that Z. A. Bhutto had been all too human would have been a major blunder: Pakistan's powerful Islamist sector, which already hated the secular Bhutto, should by no means be given gratuitous information about his extramarital fornications. Psychologically, Benazir appears to have been unable to admit to any imperfection in the father she so idolized. "Of course, she was madly in love with her father," more than one of her friends has stated in interviews, and however one takes this comment, she was certainly far too heavily invested in him, both professionally and emotionally, to wish to acknowledge any of his character flaws. In any case Bhutto's powerful sexuality was indivisible from his political charisma; one could hardly have existed without the other.

When Benazir was ten and her sister, Sanam, seven, they were sent to boarding school at Murree, a mountain town that had been one of the famous hill stations of the Raj. Here, again, Benazir was educated by nuns. She was at Murree when, in 1965, the first Indo-Pakistani war over Kashmir broke out. At the time of partition in 1947, Kashmir's Hindu raja had brought Kashmir into India, despite the opposition of the Muslim majority population. From that time to this Kashmir has been disputed territory, the focus of paranoia on both sides of the border, and the cause of three wars between the two nations.

Zulfikar Ali Bhutto — who in 1963, at the age of thirty-five, had achieved his ambition of becoming foreign minister — strongly believed that the Muslim-majority Kashmir was an integral part of Pakistan; in fact he was far more hawkish on this subject than the rather moderate Ayub. Disturbed by reports that India was surging ahead in the arms race and by the apparent strengthening of ties between India and the United States, Bhutto masterminded Operation Gibraltar, an attempt to foment an uprising in Kashmir by infiltrating Pakistani guerrillas into the region, disguised as locals. The hope was that native Kashmiris would join the guerrillas in resistance until the whole of Kashmir could be liberated from India. The operation was badly executed and led to a confrontation between India and Pakistan that has become known as the Second Kashmir War, a conflict that lasted five months and caused thousands of casualties.

The road to Kashmir ran directly through Murree, and the nuns who taught Benazir and Sanam feared that Indian troops would use it to invade their country. The students at the Convent of Jesus and Mary had air raid practices and constructed bomb shelters. Benazir, only twelve years old at the time, already showed the remarkable fighting spirit that would later distinguish her political career: she quite enjoyed the prospect of being kidnapped, discussing it excitedly with her sister and their schoolmates. In the end the war was stopped by a United Nations–mandated cease-fire. Cease-fire negotiations were held in Tashkent (in modern Uzbekistan), where the so-called Tashkent Declaration was signed on January 10, 1966.

The war had been fairly equal on both sides, though by the end the Pakistanis were running low on ammunition. The Pakistani press, however, painted every moderately successful move by their army as a glorious victory, and when Ayub Khan agreed at Tashkent with Indian prime minister Lal Bahadur Shastri that preconflict borders would be reestablished, the hawks, led by Bhutto, loudly complained that Ayub had squandered at the negotiating table all they had gained in battle. Bhutto resigned from the cabinet and, in 1967, joined with a group of political allies, all disenchanted with Ayub and military rule, to found a new political party, the Pakistan People's Party. Meetings took place in the house Zulfikar had built for his family, 70 Clifton, Karachi.

The PPP's motto was simple: "Islam is our faith, democracy is our policy, socialism is our economy. All power to the People." It pledged to provide every Pakistani, however poor, with *roti, kapra aur makan* — bread, clothes, and housing. Kashmir was part of the agenda: it was, according to the PPP, an integral part of Pakistan and must be "liberated."

Bhutto started out as one among equals, but as the party developed he elbowed his way to the top. "It was already a tradition in the short history of Pakistani politics for noted opposition figures to found their own parties rather than play a secondary role in someone else's organization," one historian of the country has written, adding that "the cult of personality and lack of party strength and durability contributed to the fractious history of Pakistani politics then as it does now."[4]

The PPP's populist message rapidly gained followers, and Bhutto himself was soon on a roll. He toured the country during 1968, denouncing Ayub and beating the democratic drum. The PPP, he told the crowds, would dismantle the feudalism that still clung to the country, redistribute land, and create a classless society. Bhutto's fiery speeches had thrilled the country during the Kashmir war three years previously; now that same impassioned rhetoric filled his countrymen with a new hope for the future.

Ayub had organized a nationwide celebration to mark his decade in rule, which he self-flatteringly dubbed a "Decade of Revolution." But now, instead of getting the adulation he sought, he was being heckled by crowds of PPP supporters. Rioting broke out in urban centers. When Bhutto arrived in Lahore late in 1968 he was greeted almost as a messiah, with a crowd of one hundred thousand at the train station to meet him, his worshippers literally hanging from the rafters. Ayub finally decided that his only recourse was to arrest this troublemaker. On November 12 Bhutto was taken into custody, along with his PPP colleagues Dr. Mubashir Hasan and Mumtaz Ali Bhutto. They were imprisoned for three months in Mianwali Prison on the Indus River. Their actions, however, had fatally weakened the rule of Ayub Khan, who on March 25, 1969, handed the reins of power to the army commander in chief, General Yahya Khan.

No matter what new drama beset the family, the Bhutto children were never allowed to forget their studies, and Benazir was now cramming for her O-level examinations (Pakistan's educational system is modeled on the British one). It could not have been easy to concentrate on schoolwork at that moment, but she was aware of how terribly important it was to her father that she excel academically and attend a world-class university, and

so she persisted. Zulfikar's plan was for her to attend Radcliffe
College at Harvard for a BA degree, then go to Oxford and read
"Greats" (the course of study now known as Philosophy, Politics and Economics — PPE), and then, possibly, take a postgraduate course at Oxford. At the end of all this preparation she was
to come home and join the Pakistani diplomatic corps. It was
a plan Benazir saw no reason to argue with, as it fit in exactly
with her own interests and preferred lifestyle. To set her on this
road, Zulfikar continued to direct her O-level preparation from
his jail cell, where he was being held in solitary confinement. "I
know you read a great deal," he wrote to her, "but you should
read a little more literature and history. You have all the books
you need. Read about Napoleon Bonaparte, the most complete
man in modern history. Read about the American Revolution
and about Abraham Lincoln. Read *Ten Days That Shook the
World* by John Reed. Read about Bismarck and Lenin, Atatürk
and Mao Tse-tung. Read the history of India from ancient
times. And above all read the history of Islam."[5]

Zulfikar's choice of great historic figures is singularly revealing: with the exception of Lincoln, each of these "great men"
was a famous authoritarian. And considering Zulfikar's own behavior during the war over the secession of East Pakistan three
years later, it is doubtful whether he himself took many lessons
from Abraham Lincoln. Lincoln kept the American union together; Zulfikar Ali Bhutto was one of principal forces that tore
the fragile and perhaps always doomed Pakistani union apart.

His exhortation to Benazir to read more literature and history is an interesting one. Benazir would turn out to be a woman
of action rather than an intellectual, and her reading tended to
fall into two categories: the utilitarian and the pleasurable. She
enjoyed the gossipy *Hello!* magazine, and more than one visitor
to 70 Clifton has been amused by the sight of Benazir's book-
shelf, carefully preserved since her youthful tenure there, on

which her well-thumbed copies of lowbrow Mills & Boon romance novels still preside. And in the last years of her life, an old college friend visiting her at her Dubai mansion would be startled by "her little library stuffed with paperbacks, titles such as *Facial Workout, The Little Book of Stress, Eat to Beat Your Age,* Deepak Chopra's *How to Know God.*" "For an Oxford and Harvard graduate," Benazir's classmate Amy Wilentz continued, "she was unembarrassed by her addiction to bestsellers, blockbusters and psychobabble books," and she quoted Benazir as saying, "For all the lows in my life, those self-help books helped me survive, I can tell you. There's a focus on the present; don't worry about tomorrow."[6]

It was in this spirit that Benazir sat for her O-levels in December 1968, with the city in full crisis mode. The best way she could help her beleaguered father, she knew, was to excel in the arena he had chosen for her. To keep the students safe from the anti-Ayub riots that were rocking the city, the exams were administered in the Vatican embassy, in a secure neighborhood not far from her home. She did well in the tests, and Zulfikar determined she would begin at Radcliffe in the fall. As she was only sixteen, however, the powers-that-be at Radcliffe decreed that she should wait another year. This was just not good enough for Zulfikar, who from his prison cell, and now on a hunger strike, contacted his friend John Kenneth Galbraith, the economist who had been US ambassador to India and was now a professor at Harvard. The necessary strings were pulled, and Benazir's admission was cleared. Again, that resemblance to the Kennedy family: Zulfikar micromanaged his children's education and progress through life as assiduously as Joseph P. Kennedy had done — or at least he did until his premature downfall.

BEFORE THE SIXTEEN-YEAR-OLD Benazir left for America in the fall of 1969, her father had warned her that she might see things there that would shock her, and on arrival she found that this was so. The most shocking thing of all was her fellow students' ignorance of her country. Many of them had not even heard of Pakistan, and among those who had, few could place it on a map. If they were told it was next to India, that cleared up quite a bit (this was, after all, the sixties, and India was a favorite stop on the hippie trail), but the basic facts of Pakistani history and geography — that it had come into being only twenty-three years earlier, had at that time the largest Muslim population in the world, and was comprised of two wings, West and East, separated by a thousand miles of hostile India — were largely unknown even to America's best and brightest students. That Pakistan was supposed to be an important American ally against communism, and that the average American knew nothing about this and cared less, was an additional blow to the extreme national pride with which Benazir had been raised.

She was also shocked, at least initially, by what she perceived as the rigors of daily life in a nominally egalitarian, nonhierarchical society. To say that she had been surrounded by servants from birth is an understatement: the family retainers of Pakistan's great feudal families lead lives more reminiscent of those of Russian serfs than of American or European servants.[1] Before Benazir's arrival at Radcliffe, recounted her fellow student, the future writer Anne Fadiman, "she had never cooked a meal, washed a blouse, walked more than a block without being picked up by a chauffeur, or lifted a ringing telephone. She cried most of her first semester."[2] Like her father, who on his first night in his Los Angeles boardinghouse had wondered who was going to draw his bath, Benazir was unable to perform the smallest household task. She quickly learned many of these skills, of course, and was proud of the new competence that was not the least of what she took away from her years abroad. But even after four years in America she never shed her characteristic *de haut en bas* arrogance, a relic of her feudal upbringing and the Bhuttos' propensity to see themselves as royalty. Four years later, when she was at Oxford, her Indian friend Shyam Bhatia, now a well-known journalist, noted that "Benazir at university epitomized the classic spoilt rich girl from a Third World country. She was self-obsessed, liked to have her own way, and her temper tantrums were legendary." Bhatia went on to quote another Oxford student who had visited the family in Pakistan: "'When Pinkie loses her temper, she throws ashtrays like flying saucers at the servants.'"[3]

But if these comments make Benazir sound difficult and unpopular, that was very far from being the case. Most of her new friends found her a galvanic, energizing presence, intellectually curious, humorous, passionately engaged in college life. "She was funny," Fadiman has said, "*very* funny."[4] "She loved that she was relatively anonymous," recalls her Harvard roommate, Yolanda Kodrzycki. "She was exotic but she could blend in. She liked to hang out with people who weren't very political. It was an escape — she was so much in the limelight in Pakistan."[5] She became a campus tour guide and the social secretary of her dorm, Eliot House. She soon shed her distinctly uncool *shalwar kameez* — the traditional Pakistani garment she favored in Karachi—for jeans and T-shirts. Dating, though, was not an option for her. "I think that in a sense she lived vicariously through her friends," says Kodrzycki, "and was very intensely interested in her friends' love lives."[6]

Benazir found surrogate parents in Galbraith and his wife; their son Peter Galbraith was also at Harvard and would attend Oxford during Benazir's time there as well. In his future career Peter would prove perhaps Benazir Bhutto's most important friend, the kind of ideal American connection Zulfikar had sent her to Harvard to meet. (It was to be Peter's intervention, in 1983, that secured Benazir's freedom after five years in custody.)

The year 1969 was a heady time to be at a great American university—perhaps the headiest time ever. The antiwar movement was in full swing, as was the sexual revolution; Benazir was exposed to ideas, assumptions, and ways of thinking that had never quite permeated even the relatively liberated milieu she inhabited in Pakistan. As a fellow Asian she vocally sympathized with the Vietnamese and expressed resentment at American incursions into their country. She had opposed the war even before she arrived in the United States; once there, caught up in the momentum of the times, she marched on Washington and joined a Moratorium Day protest on Boston Common. The women's movement was reaching a crescendo: in 1970, shortly after Benazir's arrival in America, the seminal *Sexual Politics,* by Kate Millett, was published and became, in Benazir's words, "the campus bible." Yolanda Kodrzycki remembers that Benazir did not swallow Millett's message whole; in fact, "she was very critical of the women's movement . . . She had this view that women were becoming unwomanly in the women's movement. She felt that women were losing the sense of what it meant to be a woman."[7] Student rap sessions in this period of second-wave feminism centered around new models for combining work and marriage, but Benazir was always aware that the issues she would face as a relatively liberated and secular woman in a traditional, patriarchal culture were very different from those that would confront her American friends. As Kodrzycki noticed, she was definitely interested in attractive men, but she was probably less concerned, even then, with marriage than with the career in public life she was eagerly planning. But she would have realized that a husband was an indispensable accoutrement in the program she had mapped out for herself: in Pakistani society, a single woman's legal rights were limited and her prestige low.

If Benazir's Harvard friends knew nothing about Pakistan when she arrived, they were soon to learn a great deal, for a tragedy was unfolding before the world's eyes, one in which Benazir's famous father played a starring, if not a heroic, role. On December 7, 1970, Pakistan held its first general election since independence, with results that might have been predicted. The geographic division of the country was bizarre and probably would never have been workable over the long run. West Pakistan was made up of the Punjab, by far the dominant province; Sindh; North-West Frontier Province; and Balochistan. East Pakistan, separated from the West by a thousand miles of India, was East Bengal. (West Bengal was *in* India.) The two parts of Pakistan were distinct ethnically, socially, linguistically. East Pakistan was geographically smaller but had a slightly larger population. West Pakistan had the economic and military edge: with the breakup of the Raj, it had inherited the military infrastructure. The Punjab had been the "sword arm" of the Raj, and the higher echelons of the army were from that part of the country; the city of Rawalpindi, in West Pakistan, was home to the army's general headquarters. The state bureaucracy, too, was overwhelmingly situated in West rather than East Pakistan.

The East Pakistanis felt, with some justification, that the western half of the country treated their half like a colony. Each year some three billion rupees ($300 million) were transferred from East to West Pakistan and spent on consumption and capital investment in the West. When funds and resources were allocated nationally, the East inevitably got the short end of the stick. More than that, Urdu and English had been named the official languages of Pakistan, while Bengali, the language of East Pakistan, was ignored. In 1968–9 a major uprising had taken place, in which the East Pakistani Awami League, led by Sheikh Mujibur Rahman, presented a very reasonable Six-Point Plan demanding increased autonomy for the beleaguered East.

In the 1970 elections, West Pakistan saw the Islamist Jamaat-e-Islami confront Bhutto's PPP, while in East Pakistan the Awami League emerged as the leading party. When votes were counted, it turned out that the inevitable had happened: in West Pakistan, the PPP had done best, but the Awami League had swept East Pakistan, winning 160 out of 162 seats in East Pakistan and an absolute majority in the National Assembly. According to parliamentary principles, the Awami League's Sheikh Mujib should be the leader of Pakistan.

This was most definitely not an outcome Zulfikar Ali Bhutto was prepared to accept. He refused to admit that Mujib had any right to lead all of Pakistan, contending that the majority parties of the country's two wings — the PPP and the Awami League — should share power. Mujib did not agree. Bhutto, passionately intransigent, threatened to "break the legs" of any PPP members who took their elected places in the new National Assembly. The stalemate was on.

The new Assembly was supposed to draft a new constitution, reestablishing civilian government after twelve years of military rule. But the inability of Mujib and Bhutto to come to an agreement made Yahya Khan's role in the transfer of power more important. Bhutto and Mujib spent two inconclusive months haggling over the details of the new constitution, with Mujib threatening to demand virtual autonomy for East

Pakistan if he did not get his way and Bhutto cementing alliances with the military. Tehmina Durrani, wife of Bhutto's on-again, off-again political crony Mustafa Khar and daughter of the governor of the State Bank, has claimed that Bhutto secretly tried to strong-arm her father, with physical threats, to withdraw state assets from East Pakistan. With growing unrest in East Pakistan, including mass protests, civil war was suddenly a frightening possibility.

Then, at midnight on March 25, 1971, the Pakistani military launched Operation Searchlight, a campaign of brutal repression in East Pakistan. "This revolting campaign," writes historian Anatol Lieven, "was the most terrible blot on the entire record of the Pakistani army, and was made possible by old and deep-seated racial contempt by the Punjabi and Pathan soldiery for the Bengalis, whom they also regarded as not true Muslims but crypto-Hindus."[8] Operation Searchlight was masterminded and led by General Tikka Khan, who earned the title of "Butcher of Bengal" for his ruthless crackdown not only on separatists and agitators but also on many thousands of Bengalis who had no involvement in politics whatever. The offensive started at the University of Dacca, with a massive tank assault against student dormitories; students and intellectuals were targeted throughout Operation Searchlight. The army used rape systematically, as an instrument of warfare. Mujibur Rahman was thrown into jail and the Awami League outlawed. In the East, separatist leaders proclaimed the independent republic of Bangladesh.

Refugees fleeing the horror in East Pakistan began pouring over the border into India at a rapid rate: by the end of the conflict, their number would total something like ten million. The killings hit genocidal levels, with Hindus residing in East Pakistan — there were some ten million of them — bearing the brunt of the attacks. Images of the carnage in the press shocked the world, the horror compounded by the deadly tropical cyclone that had struck the Bengali coast just before the war, killing between three and five hundred thousand people. Bangladesh, in 1971, was the most terrible place on earth.

Zulfikar Ali Bhutto unapologetically supported the military action, laying out his views in a tract called *The Great Tragedy,* in which he rather surprisingly referred to Bangladeshi separatism as "the nightmare of fascism."[9] In late November India, with its vast military machine, came into the war on the side of Bangladesh. This spelled the end for the Pakistani army, which collapsed in disarray two weeks later.

In December 1971 Bhutto headed for New York to present the West Pakistani case before the UN Security Council, and he summoned Benazir to join him at the luxurious Pierre Hotel, his usual quarters when visiting New York. Here she got a crash course in international crisis politics when Zulfikar asked her to man the telephone in his suite. She fielded calls from Henry Kissinger as well as from the heads of the Soviet, Chinese, and American delegations to the UN. (The American delegation happened to be led by George H. W. Bush.) Her father instructed her, she later recounted, to interrupt the meetings for maximum effect: "If the Soviets are here, tell me the Chinese are calling. If the Americans are here, tell me that the Russians are on the line or the Indians. And don't tell anyone who really is here. One of the fundamental lessons of diplomacy is to create doubt: never lay all your cards on the table."[10] It was Benazir's first experience of the excitement of power politics; she was thrilled and galvanized.

As usual, she saw only the glitter as she watched her father's performance at the UN, but it was clear to the international cast of players assembled there that Z. A. Bhutto was one hundred percent behind Tikka Khan's cruel offensive. Undersecretary-General Brian Urquhart, who found Bhutto "intelligent, arrogant, charming, and unpredictable,"[11] recalls the scene:

I called Bhutto at the Pierre Hotel and explained what had happened. He flew into a great passion and said over and over again, "The Pakistan Army will fight to the last man and the last round." I asked Bhutto if he really thought the Pierre Hotel in New York was the best place to fight to the last man and the last round in Dacca. He began to laugh and said that of course we must pass the instrument of surrender to the Indians. On December 9 Pakistan accepted the cease-fire. The nation of Bangladesh was born.[12]

Yahya Khan would look back bitterly on the tragedy years later. "It was Bhutto, not Mujib," he reflected, "who broke Pakistan. Bhutto's stance in 1971 and his stubbornness harmed Pakistan's solidarity much more than Sheikh Mujib's six-point demand. It was his high ambitions and rigid stance that led to rebellion in East Pakistan."[13] But at the time this was not evident to the world, and it was certainly not evident to the blinkered Benazir, who found herself in the position of having to passionately defend her father's motives and actions to her American friends; they were horrified by the news reports and photographs coming out of Bangladesh. Zulfikar and Nusrat sent Benazir articles from government-controlled Pakistani newspapers that claimed Western news reports were exaggerated, part of a Zionist plot in fact. In her naïveté or, more probably, her unwillingness to credit anything that did not reflect well on her beloved father, she believed them, and tried unsuccessfully to impart this point of view to her fellow students and even to the professors at Harvard: Anne Fadiman remembers her lecturing a professor, Michael Walzer, who had dared to criticize West Pakistani policies in a class. Several years later she even embarked on a remarkably ill-advised attempt to persuade the faculty of Oxford to award her father an honorary degree, still not realizing the extent to which he had been tainted in the eyes of the world. In her autobiography she would admit that she had been unforgivably ignorant at that time, but she would never place any of the blame on Zulfikar. Her retrospective comments are revealing:

> Instead of working with my father and the representatives of West Pakistan to write a new constitution acceptable to both wings of Pakistan, Mujib instigated an independence movement to sever East Pakistan, or East Bengal, from the western federation completely. Time and again my father appealed to Sheikh Mujib to keep Pakistan intact, to work together with him, a fellow civilian, to oust the military rule of Yahya. But instead of showing flexibility and agreeing to what was a political necessity, Mujib showed an obstinacy the logic of which to this day defies me.[14]

With his lawyer's policy of never admitting a fault, Zulfikar blamed everyone but himself for the horrors of the war and the loss of half the country. In a bizarre television interview at Heathrow Airport in December 1971, as he returned from New York to Pakistan to claim the presidency, he asserted that the people of Pakistan had elected him "as their undisputed and chosen leader" a year previously, and he refused — as he always would — to accept the loss of East Pakistan as permanent. "Temporary phenomena are not realities," he insisted. "Realities are studied in history. And historically the concept of Pakistan, the idea of Pakistan, cannot perish like this."[15] Fine rhetoric, but "history" was very thin in the case of Pakistan: the nation had only twenty-three years of history behind it when it broke up.

Tainted he might have been in the world's eyes, but when Z. A. Bhutto assumed the presidency of Pakistan — which now meant just West Pakistan — on December 20, 1971, he was a hero to the majority of his people. After thirteen years of military rule, having a democratically elected leader was something

to celebrate, and cries of *"Jiye, Bhutto!"*—"Long live Bhutto!"—
rang through the streets.

The Americans didn't trust him for a moment. Since the
1940s they had been handing over billions of dollars in military
aid to Pakistan in the deluded hope that the new nation would
prove a staunch ally against communism. Pakistan had spent the
money on an arsenal hugely disproportionate to its overall budget, but the enemy its leaders had in mind was not the American
bugbear, Mao's China, but another, even closer neighbor: India,
which they hated and feared — a fact of which American leaders
had been made painfully aware both in 1965 and in 1971. Nevertheless, the Americans felt far more comfortable dealing with
army officers, with whom they had a mutual understanding,
than with populist politicians. Now, here was a declared socialist as president of Pakistan — in a Mao cap, no less! — promising
his people that they would no longer be the Americans' toadies,
aligning his country with the Chinese and Soviets, and propos-
ing himself as the leader of a potentially powerful Third World
coalition. His charisma and popularity made the White House
and the Pentagon very nervous indeed. Henry Kissinger's mem-
oirs express this nervousness nicely: "Elegant, eloquent, subtle,
Bhutto was at last a representative who would be able to com-
pete with the Indian leaders for public attention. The legacy of
distrust engendered by his flamboyant demeanor and occasionally cynical conduct haunted Bhutto within our government. I
found him brilliant, charming, of global stature in his percep-
tions."[16]

At the outset of his presidency, Bhutto promised an end to
the country's endemic nepotism and cronyism. "I have no relations, I have no family," he declared in a major public address
on inauguration day. "My family is the people of Pakistan. My
children are the people of Pakistan."[17] Yet one of his first acts
in office was to appoint as governor of Sindh his cousin Mumtaz Ali Bhutto, the family patriarch and an even bigger land-

owner than he was. And while Zulfikar might have told the crowds that his children were the people of Pakistan, his bio- logical children were still receiving the best possible education in preparation for high-profile careers in public service. Of the four of them only Shah Nawaz, who did not seem to possess his siblings' academic abilities, did not attend Harvard, going instead to the American college in Leysin, Switzerland, one of the most expensive and luxurious schools on the globe. Bena- zir was slated to move on to Oxford after graduating from Har- vard. ("She adored her father, went to Oxford to please him," re- calls one Oxford friend, "though she really loved and felt more at home in America than England."[18]) Now, as the eldest child and the only one already at university, she was chosen to accom- pany her father to India, where he was to sign the Simla accords with Indira Gandhi, putting a legal end to the Bangladesh war and negotiating the release of ninety-three thousand Pakistani prisoners of war and the return of captured Pakistani territory.

For the first time in her life, Benazir was thrust into the spotlight, and to her surprise she found that it showed her to distinct advantage. In news films of the period she can be seen following her father and being introduced to the powerful peo- ple assembled at the old hill station: she is pretty, elegant, rather demure. (Her father had warned her to show no emotion, ei- ther positive or negative, lest onlookers draw conclusions about the progress of the negotiations.) Nice-looking, but in no way showy. The inordinate attention she attracted is hard to explain. Crowds gathered around her in the street, cheering, following her, literally stopping traffic. She even became something of a fashion cynosure — odd, since in these films she never seems to be wearing anything particularly eye-catching. The members of the Pakistani delegation were at a loss to explain the phenom- enon. Benazir herself offered a plausible reason: "I symbolized a new generation. I had never been an Indian. I had been born in independent Pakistan. I was free of the complexes and prejudices which had torn Indians and Pakistanis apart in the bloody trauma of partition."[19] Kodrzycki, who saw her when she returned to Harvard, thought that the Simla experience was "the big turning point," the moment Benazir fell in love with political life. "She definitely liked the attention, she definitely liked talking to the media."[20] She was more than just an attractive girl; she had, it turned out, star quality. It was the first time she had been made aware of that fact.

Z. A. Bhutto quickly set to work to enact some of the reforms he had promised during his feverish campaign. In 1972 Pakistan's banks, insurance companies, and major industries were nationalized. Although neither Zulfikar or, later, Benazir would admit it, this move did not improve Pakistan's economic plight, for it led to an alarming level of capital flight and a serious dip in investment. Ayub's land reforms were extended, with ownership ceilings of 150 acres of irrigated and 300 acres of unirrigated land. This looked good on paper, but in practice the great landowners — Z. A. Bhutto included — simply transferred legal ownership of land packages to various relatives and retainers, never relinquishing true control over them. (When Bhutto died, his family would inherit 12,000 acres near Larkana.) The economy stagnated throughout his tenure. A new constitution was drafted under the aegis of the lawyer Mian Mahmud Ali Kasuri, which replaced the current system, in which the president had nearly absolute power, with a parliamentary one on the British model, and Bhutto duly resigned as president and took office as prime minister. Having no wish, however, to be put out of power as easily as prime ministers were in Britain, with a simple vote of no confidence, he meddled with the laws to make that process more cumbersome. He also limited the power of the judiciary and made it legal for the government to dissolve political parties. In Pakistan the army, like the intelligence services, is a formidable power in its own right and has always functioned quite independently of any civilian government: unable to control it, Bhutto left the military high command to its own devices — one of his greatest mistakes.

While outwardly pursuing his nonalignment strategy, Bhutto was still applying plenty of pressure on the United States to continue its military aid, which had slowed to a trickle in the wake of the Bangladesh war. The Americans now realized that whatever arms they supplied to Pakistan were far more likely to be used against India than against communist China or the Soviet Union. The fall of Nixon in 1974 and the change of regime in the United States after 1976, when Jimmy Carter succeeded Gerald Ford and Kissinger finally left power, were also significant, and at that time the US Congress began introducing legislation that would restrict military aid to countries that had or were developing the nuclear bomb. Bhutto was surreptitiously but determinedly supporting work on a Pakistani bomb, abetted by the metallurgist A. Q. Khan, who had stolen designs for a uranium enrichment facility from the Netherlands. The announcement of Indian nuclear tests in May 1974 was devastating to Pakistani morale, and it was now not a question of whether Pakistan would develop a bomb but how fast it would be able to do so. As far back as 1965, Bhutto had said that if India developed a bomb, "we will eat grass, even go hungry, but we will get one of our own. We have no other choice."[21] The secret machinations over nuclear intelligence would continue during Benazir's two administrations, when she herself would reportedly play a cloak-and-dagger game with Pakistan's ally North Korea.

Through all of this, Zulfikar continued living in his usual regal manner, even upping the ante to suit his new status as a world leader. Tehmina Durrani has described his spectacular dinner parties, each one "a major event for Pakistan's social and cultural elite. Bhutto was expert at the finer points of cuisine, and he dictated every detail of the menu. He loved French food and was a connoisseur of fine wines and selected with great care. He personally chose the china and cutlery. He inspected the attire and procedures of the retinue of servants. He even supervised the floral arrangements."[22] Bhutto's multifarious enemies observed his grandiosity with knowing smiles, referring to him privately as the Raja of Larkana.

He lived like a raja, and he ran the country like one, too. He used the intelligence agencies to spy on political rivals; he controlled the media, making sure that his own image was always front and center and that nothing unflattering to him appeared in print or on television. He utterly refused to share power, within the PPP and without, and serious debate was crushed. Any potential rival was seen as a threat, and eventually Bhutto took to eliminating such threats by appointing relatives, cronies, and dependents to important positions within the party and in his administration — the traditional Pakistani method, and one that Benazir adopted without hesitation when she in turn came to power. Nominally, Bhutto was a socialist. But there was little genuine change in "socialist" Pakistan.

BENAZIR'S ARRIVAL AT Oxford in the fall of 1973 was very different from her introduction to Harvard. She was no longer a shy teenager from an obscure Third World country, but a prime minister's daughter, and a beautiful, confident one at that: a star, and remembered as such by the numerous friends she made during her years in England. "Flitting between Oxford and London, where the Pakistani High Commissioner had invited her to treat his residence as a second home," her friend Shyam Bhatia recalled, "she was extremely glamorous and brought a zing of excitement to our day-to-day lives as university students. It did not seem obvious at the time, but now, looking back, Benazir seemed to be almost bubble-wrapped in a kind of all-encompassing innocence and that added to her appeal."[1] She drove an eye-catching little yellow MG, a present from her father upon her graduation from Harvard. Christopher Hitchens, who met her in England in 1975, remembered her as "a topaz-eyed slip of a thing, with a tremendous social circle and a famous father at the zenith of his power." His impression, he wrote, "had been of a pampered favorite daughter playing at a little politics and contact-making before going back to be one of Daddy's advisers."[2]

Benazir entered the women's college Lady Margaret Hall (most Oxford colleges were not yet coeducational in 1973) and embarked on a three-year degree in "Greats." Her social life was at least as important to her as her academic career, and that was perhaps as it should be, for Oxford, like Harvard, was preeminently a place to make connections. Shyam Bhatia would later recall "her desire to be liked, to be popular, and for that she was prepared to be all things to all people. This would become a recurrent theme in her later years too, explaining why she could be equally at ease with Marxists and capitalists, Indians and Israelis, fundamentalists and liberal democrats, Chinese, Australians, in fact any one on the planet."[3] She was also, he concedes, "generous to a fault."[4] She happily treated her friends to meals, trips to London in the MG, birthday celebrations.

It was almost certainly the happiest, most carefree time of her life. The roller-coaster ride her family had been on for the past few years appeared to have leveled out. Her beloved father was in his rightful place as a Great Leader. With his talents and drive, there was no reason he shouldn't stay on top for life. She herself was assured a fascinating and glamorous future, and now felt free to relax and enjoy everything Oxford had to offer. Intelligent without being an intellectual, Benazir did reasonably well in her studies, receiving a second-class degree while allowing herself plenty of time for traditional Oxford pleasures like punting on the Isis, dining on steak and mushrooms at her favorite restaurant, the Sorbonne, dancing, partying, and — according to more than one friend — enjoying the occasional flirtation. She was a fan of the Rolling Stones and the Chippendales boys. To all appearances, she was a normal — if unusually attractive — undergraduate.

Benazir finished her degree in three years and stayed on for an extra year's postgraduate study, during which time she was elected to one of the most coveted positions at the university: the presidency of the Oxford Union, the famous debating society that had launched so many political careers. Peter Galbraith, who had also moved on to Oxford after Harvard, remembers her as looking "*very* regal in her office."[5] Benazir's father had encouraged her to stand for election to this prestigious office, only warning her that "you have to do your best but the result must be accepted in good grace"[6]—a caveat of which she did not seem to perceive the irony.

Her natural gifts as a public speaker were honed during the four years in which she was a member of the Union. "I was drawn by the art of debate," she later wrote, shrewdly noting that "the power of oratory had always been a great force on the Asian subcontinent where so many were illiterate. Millions had been swayed by the words of Mahatma Gandhi, Jawaharlal Nehru, Mohammad Ali Jinnah and, indeed, my father."[7] She was widely admired for her oratorical panache, but her core political values, then as later, were hard to pin down. As Steven R. Weisman, the *New York Times* writer who had initially befriended Benazir at Harvard, later wrote, "As a debater, she was known for the quick, sarcastic put-down, especially when the subject was whimsical and form was prized over content."[8] Her friend Catherine Drucker, who heard her speak in the Union, remembers her as having been no more than a competent debater: "Most of what she said on political matters was the commonplace of the mild leftism of the day."[9]

Among the debates Bhutto participated in at the Oxford Union was a peculiarly significant one on whether the American president Nixon should be impeached. Peter Galbraith wrote her speech: "She tried to argue with me that all she needed to say was that Nixon should be impeached but not convicted,"[10] he remembered later, laughing. The high drama of the Watergate hearings going on across the Atlantic fascinated Benazir; here was an elected president being removed in a peaceful, legal manner, without the sinister specter of the army—a far cry from the fearsome "coup-gemony" of home.

Along with the excitement at Oxford, she continued to receive regular tutelage from her father. He arranged, for instance, to have her return to Pakistan from England in 1974 to attend the glitzy summit of Islamic heads of state he had arranged at Lahore in the name of the Organization of Islamic Cooperation. Thirty-five presidents and kings, as well as Yasir Arafat of the PLO, were assembled there, including Anwar Sadat, Muammar Qaddafi, Hafiz al-Assad, King Faisal of Saudi Arabia, and King Hussein of Jordan. Bhutto played proud host, taking advantage of the occasion to forge what would become a special relationship with rich Saudi Arabia, which subsequently floated him loans to purchase arms from the Americans. Benazir would later cite his consolidation of ties with the Gulf countries as having been of particular importance for his country.

In spite of various mistakes, particularly on the economic front, Z. A. Bhutto was a master of oratory and political symbolism, and he became increasingly popular among the common people of Pakistan, little though their own lives might have changed as a result of his token reforms. His biggest mistake, though, was not an economic misjudgment but a personal one. In 1976 the faithful General Tikka Khan left his position as army chief of staff and Bhutto was obliged to appoint a new one. Going against conventional wisdom, he skipped over five senior lieutenant generals to choose the unprepossessing, fifty-two-year-old Mohammed Zia ul-Haq.

Unlike most of the top army brass, Zia was no Anglicized, whiskey-imbibing Sandhurst man but the scion of a lower-middle-class and devoutly Muslim family. He was also, unusually for a high-ranking officer, a *muhajir* — a Muslim who had crossed over into Pakistan from a Hindu-dominated territory at partition. He had studied economics at the University of Delhi before joining the Indian Army, under the British, in 1943; later, in the early sixties, he did two years of training at Fort Leavenworth, during which time he might very possibly have forged connections with the American military establishment and the CIA.

Bhutto's surprising appointment of Zia was made on the

basis of Zia's supposed malleability: this obsequious, smarmy man would never pose a threat, everyone assured him. The weird-looking Zia appeared to have little natural authority. "I remember being startled when I saw him," Benazir wrote. "Unlike the childish image I carried of a soldier as tall and rugged with James Bond nerves of steel, the General standing in front of me was a short, nervous, ineffectual-looking man whose pomaded hair was parted in the middle and lacquered to his head. He looked more like an English cartoon villain than an inspiring military leader."[11]

Zia seemed perfectly content to present himself as a toady to the masterful Bhutto. And Bhutto, who had a cruel, even sadistic streak, was happy to treat him as such, referring to him as "Zia ul-Muck" or "Cobra Eyes." Bhutto, wrote his biographer Stanley Wolpert,

> often made Zia the butt of public ridicule, shouting at him from the head of the dinner table, "Where is my monkey-general? Come over here, Monkey!" He would pretend to pull Zia toward himself on an invisible string and then introduce him to a distinguished foreign guest, quickly dismissing him, even before Zia finished bowing, ever smiling. Sometimes Zulfi "joked" about how "funny" Zia's teeth looked, humiliating the man he had singled out for such high and powerful distinction... Zia apparently never took umbrage at such "jests," always smiling, bowing, even "thanking" his prime minister for "your such kind attention, Sir!"[12]

Tariq Ali remembers a conversation he had with Benazir at about this time.

> I said to Benazir Bhutto, "This man is going to topple your father. He is the Uriah Heep of Pakistani politics. In front of you he sort of cringes and is servile and sycophantic, but

in his head there is another plan ... Tell your father from me
that either he will be assassinated or there will be a military
coup." And she said, "Assassination, who can stop them? A
military coup, never, because General Zia is in our pocket,"
and she touched her imaginary pocket. I said, "Benazir, you
just tell your father that I said no Pakistani general is ever in
the pocket of a civilian politician."[13]

It was a direct warning that Benazir should have taken seriously, but like her father she scoffed at such worries. As she remarked later, "In our culture, one does not betray one's benefactor."[14] True in theory, but with this comment she willfully
ignored her own father's treatment of Ayub Khan, who had undoubtedly been both his benefactor and his political mentor.

But if his rough treatment at the prime minister's hands ran-
kled, Zia said nothing and bided his time. Bhutto had called for
elections to be held in March 1977, and campaign fever was getting under way. It was predicted that the PPP would win easily;
the ISI — the powerful and impenetrable Inter-Services Intelligence agency — had informed Bhutto that he could probably
count on 70 to 80 percent of the votes in the most important
regions. The opposition, in the meantime, united under the
name of the Pakistan National Alliance (PNA). A variety of
parties made up the PNA, but it was dominated by rightist and
Islamist parties and led by Maulana Mufti Mahmood, a cleric
who was chairman of the Islamist Jamaat-e-Islami party.

Benazir and her brother Murtaza, who had by now followed
her to Oxford, watched the proceedings anxiously from England. The PNA agitators were very vocal, particularly the Islamists. Bhutto's blatant secularism had always made him unpopular with a significant portion of the population. Not that
he was the first Pakistani leader of this type: Ayub and Yahya
had not been particularly devout, and indeed Jinnah himself,
the *Qaid-i-Azam,* had been a committed secularist. The na-

tion of Pakistan had been born not from an outpouring of religious feeling but from a fear, only too well founded, that in an independent India with a Hindu majority the Muslim population would be marginalized and rendered politically impotent. But something about Bhutto's special flamboyance — the Savile Row style, the open use of alcohol, the kept mistress — was particularly irksome to the Islamists, and the fact that Bhutto's mother had been a Hindu and his wife was an Iranian Shi'ite did not help his standing with them. In this area he had to walk a very fine line — as would Benazir in her turn, with rather more success.

Bhutto had done his best to appease hard-core Islamists already. The 1973 constitution had created a "Council of Islamic Ideology" to make sure that none of the nation's laws went against Islamic tenets. It also made teaching of the Koran compulsory in schools, cracked down on gambling, and organized a governmental framework for the collection of *zakat,* the required religious charitable donations. A 1974 amendment appeased the religious parties by proclaiming the heretic Ahmadiyya sect to be outside the pale of Islam. Now, with zealots in the PNA baying for his blood, Bhutto continued his appeasement policy by declaring a ban on alcohol (without, however, making any adjustment to his own habits) and changing the weekly day of rest from Sunday to Friday — although one has to wonder why, in a country with a 97 percent Muslim population, this had not happened earlier.

It was more or less a given that the PPP would win the elections, and it did, with 155 seats in the National Assembly to the PNA's 36. But many observers of the campaign, including Z. A. Bhutto's biographer, have concluded that Bhutto, unwilling to take any chances whatsoever on the outcome, rigged certain local elections and set up, via the ISI, an "election cell" that would help guarantee a favorable outcome by threatening opposition candidates. The backlash might have been fomented by politi-

cal enemies, but there was real outrage, with PNA-directed uprisings spread through Pakistan, creating chaos and paralyzing
entire cities. Bhutto tried to quell the rage by soothing Islamist
sensibilities, introducing what he called "complete prohibition"
throughout the country: nightclubs and movie houses were
shut down, as were gambling venues and bars. He also agreed to
hold reelections for the forty seats that were said to have been
stolen; Saudi Arabia, his new best friend, stepped in and helped
to broker an agreement between the PPP and the PNA. But just
as it seemed a compromise might be reached, ominous signals
began emanating from the army chief.

On the evening of July 4, Mustafa Khar met with Zia ul-
Haq and was surprised by a change in the oily general's demeanor. "General Zia suddenly seems to have opinions of his
own," Khar informed his wife. "The man was disagreeing with
some of the plans we were putting forward. His attitude change
means that he is being manipulated by bigger powers. I warned
Mr. Bhutto. Something's brewing."[15] Then, in the early hours of
the next morning, Zia abruptly seized power, proclaiming martial law throughout the country. He immediately removed the
nuclear program from civilian control, authorizing the military
takeover of Kahuta, home of the nuclear research laboratories.
He suspended the constitution, dissolved the National Assembly, fired all ministers and governors, and imprisoned — or, in
the euphemistic terminology of tyranny, placed under "protective custody" — Bhutto and his PPP associates, along with some
senior PNA leaders for good measure.

ENERAL ZIA PLEDGED to hold elections within
ninety days, under a plan he dubbed, ironically enough,
Operation Fairplay. In fact, he would reign as sole dictator for the next eleven years, never relinquishing his hold on
power until death unexpectedly removed him from the scene.
During his tenure, Pakistan, which has undergone so many
troubles and vicissitudes, reached what was probably the nadir
of its history.

As far as Benazir Bhutto is concerned, these eleven years
were undoubtedly her finest. They were years of anguish and
suffering for her and her family, but they proved her to be a
woman of extraordinary resilience, determination, and, most
of all, courage; like her father, she turned out to possess leadership gifts of a very high order. The self-serving compromises
that would blight her years in power could never have been predicted from the truly heroic defiance she displayed throughout
her dealings with the military dictatorship. When she fought
her way to the top as leader of the PPP, over the heads of the
older generation, she appeared to many to have earned the position fair and square.

It is very possible that the special treatment her father had
always given her, treatment that others perceived as having
spoiled her and given her a sense of extreme entitlement, also
helped forge a toughness that would see her through hardships

that would have defeated most people. The belief that the Bhuttos were unique, and possessed of a unique destiny, inspired in her a determination that the world should recognize and acknowledge that uniqueness. The arrogant girl was indivisible from the powerful woman who would impress the world.

She had arrived at Rawalpindi in Pakistan only a few days before the coup, having finally completed her education and celebrated its conclusion with a big twenty-fourth-birthday blowout at Oxford. The family, reunited after a long separation (and, it should be said, for the last time), planned to stay there for a few days together; then Benazir was to spend the summer working for the prime minister's office and the Inter-Provincial Council of Common Interests, go to the UN in September as part of the Pakistani delegation, and then, on her return, prepare for her foreign ministry exams.

Her eight years in America and England had given her an education in Western political theory and practice but had not, perhaps, endowed her with the requisite cynicism to comprehend a country in which the army exists independently of any civilian restraints. Benazir later recorded a conversation she had with her father as the Bhutto family sat at Rawalpindi during the early hours of July 5, waiting for the military escort to take Zulfikar away.

> "You are a student of world government," my father says to me. "Do you think Zia will hold elections?"
>
> "Yes, I do, Papa," I tell him, still full of student idealism and academic logic. "By supervising the elections himself, Zia will be able to deprive the opposition of any claim they were rigged and the pretext to start new agitations."
>
> "Don't be an idiot, Pinkie," my father says in a quiet voice. "Armies do not take over power to relinquish it. Nor do Generals commit high treason in order to hold elections and restore democratic constitutions."[1]

Z. A. Bhutto's first prison was the comfortable prime minister's rest house in the hill station of Murree, where he was taken along with several of his political cronies (or henchmen, as many deemed them). There, in spite of the glum prognosis he had outlined to Benazir, he seemed to observers to be his usual optimistic, forceful self, holding court and planning the PPP's next step. He continued to direct the Bhutto family's actions from a distance, sending Murtaza to visit his constituency in Larkana while Nusrat, Benazir, and Shah Nawaz held the fort in Karachi, meeting with PPP supporters at 70 Clifton. When floods devastated Lahore, Bhutto dispatched Murtaza and Benazir there to demonstrate the PPP's solidarity with the people's sufferings. For the first time, Benazir realized that her rudimentary Urdu was a handicap to the PPP cause, and she set about trying to learn the language in a more systematic manner.

Zia was behaving disturbingly, consolidating a program that combined military rule with Islamization according to fundamentalist principles. This was something new in Pakistan. A series of martial law orders forbade citizens to attend trade union, student union, or political party meetings, or to criticize the army in speech or writing. Socialists, intellectuals, and journalists were rounded up and arrested. A sharia council was created to make sure the country's legal code was in line with Islamic law. Five-times-a-day prayer was enforced; public eating and drinking during Ramadan were outlawed; blasphemy against the Prophet was made punishable by death. The penalty for looting was punishable by the amputation of a hand. Public floggings were staged in sports stadiums, with thousands of spectators.

Bhutto's first incarceration lasted less than a month; he was released in late July and allowed, at least for the moment, to re-enter the political arena. The outpouring of emotion among his supporters upon his release fooled Benazir, and perhaps Zulfikar, too, into a false sense of security: How could Zia dare destroy such a popular figure? Surely revolution would ensue if he were to be eliminated. A crowd of more than a million greeted him upon his homecoming to Karachi; Benazir remembered that what was "normally a half-hour trip from the train station to our home took my father ten hours. His car was dented and scratched by the time it arrived at 70 Clifton."[2] Later, when he entered Lahore, the crowds were even larger — three million, by one estimate. Benazir accompanied him to Rawalpindi, where their car was again mobbed, and addressed a group of women supporters of the PPP.

There can be no doubt that Zia was unsettled by the show of support; he even issued a warning to Benazir and her mother not to engage in political activity. The popularity of Bhutto and the PPP made it evident that they would easily triumph in elections if they were actually held. So as Bhutto communed with his people in Karachi, Lahore, and the Bhuttos' al-Murtaza compound in Larkana, Zia went to work creating the legal machinery that would bring him down for good. On August 15 the Federal Investigation Agency, now under Zia's thumb, indicted Bhutto for "direct responsibility" in the murder of Muhammad Ahmad Khan Kasuri, the father of a political opponent who was supposed to have been Bhutto's real target. On September 3, 1977, just two weeks before the election campaign was supposed to begin, army commandos entered the Bhutto home at 70 Clifton and arrested Zulfikar on a charge of murder.

It was a moment of supreme horror for the family, when any illusions that the regime had still to adhere to the nation's legal system were shattered. The murder charge was patently fabricated; Bhutto was a ruthless politician, to be sure, but no one actually believed him guilty of this particular crime. He was released on bail ten days later, when the high court justice in Lahore, by all accounts a fair and honest man, determined that the case had no legal basis. Zia, then in Iran on a public relations tour of Pakistan's Muslim allies, was outraged. "What is the Constitution?" he shouted, rhetorically, at his Iranian hosts. "It is a booklet with ten or twelve pages. I can tear them up and say that from tomorrow, we shall live under a different system. Is there anybody to stop me? Today the people will follow wherever I lead. All the politicians, including the once mighty Mr. Bhutto, will follow me with their tails wagging."[3] Zia ordered Bhutto's rearrest, but not before the latter had had time to make fiery anti-Zia speeches in Multan and Karachi. On the night of September 16, army commandoes climbed the walls of al-Murtaza in Larkana and promptly rearrested Bhutto under Martial Law Regulation 12, a rule allowing the arrest of any individual deemed by the martial law administrator (Zia himself) to be working against law, order, or martial law. One of Bhutto's last actions before his arrest was to make his wife, Nusrat, the acting chairman of the PPP.

This is a fact Benazir found awkward when she came to write her emotional account of the events, in which her own role is exaggerated and her mother's considerable one reduced to a minimum. "My mother hadn't wanted this public life," she insisted, "hadn't wanted to assume the leadership of the PPP while my father was in prison."[4] But the inconvenient truth appears to be that it was not Benazir whom Zulfikar named as his political heir, nor even her brother Murtaza, who would also later attempt to assume the mantle, but Nusrat.

Male children appeared more threatening than females to Bhutto's political enemies, and he would take no risks: knowing that the military authorities would have few qualms about disposing of them, he ordered Murtaza and Shah Nawaz to leave for Europe immediately. Murtaza headed for England, while Shah returned to his college in Switzerland. Neither of them would ever see their father again. Sanam proceeded to Harvard. According to Benazir's account, Zulfikar agreed to her staying on in Pakistan, albeit with reluctance, for she, too, would inevitably be made a target by the regime.

Zulfikar was moved from prison to prison in an effort to keep his location a secret from the public. First it was Sukkur, then Karachi, then Kot Lakhpat Jail in Lahore. Nusrat and Benazir continued to contest the elections for the PPP. At the age of twenty-four, Benazir — a polished speaker thanks to her years in the Oxford Union, but still politically naive and, above all, unaccustomed to the tremendous, surging Pakistani crowds — began her public career, delivering her first major speech at a huge public meeting in Faisalabad and following it up with others throughout the Punjab. With not only Zulfikar but also many other PPP notables in detention, Benazir and Nusrat were trying to fill in as many gaps as possible. Then, in Sahiwal on September 29, police surrounded the house Benazir was staying in and informed its owners that it had been made a sub-jail. Benazir and her hosts would be detained there for the next fifteen days. During that time, Zia canceled the elections.

All bets were now off as the unpredictable diktats of martial law replaced the legal framework to which Zia had so far been pretending to adhere. Benazir, after all, had not been breaking any law when she was arrested, not even one of the "emergency" martial law measures. Her arrest was the signal that Zia felt confident to break free of constitutional guarantees; with power, he was gaining confidence. She could no longer depend on legal or constitutional rights; there were no safe places.

Z. A. Bhutto's murder trial began on October 24 and lasted five months. Former US attorney general Ramsey Clark attended it, later describing the proceedings not as a trial of murder but the murder of a trial, a kangaroo court of the most egregious kind.

> The acting Chief Justice's conduct would make Judge Julius Hoffman in the Chicago 7 trial a model of decorum. He publicly commented on Bhutto's "guilt" outside the courtroom before conviction. His prejudice is spread through his

145-page decision . . . The evidence presented against Bhutto,
even if believed, would not support a verdict of guilt . . . The
Chief Justice was selected by General Zia who had removed
his predecessor. Four of his associates were appointed by
General Zia.[5]

The only evidence against Bhutto was hearsay, coming from extremely unreliable sources—men who had been arrested and
probably tortured, then released in order to give the desired testimony. The chief justice, Maulvi Mushtaq, was an old enemy
of Bhutto's and a pal of Zia's; he appeared to enjoy abusing and
humiliating the defendant. Judges who had previously released
Bhutto on bail were dismissed from service.

Benazir, who had been released from detention after elections were safely canceled, attended the trial whenever possible,
appalled by the way the proceedings were conducted. She still
retained enough faith in Pakistan's vestigial ties to the British legal system to believe that her father must inevitably be acquitted, especially when the ballistics report clearly demonstrated
that the killing could not have been committed in the manner
that the prosecution claimed. Again, Zulfikar had to tell her the
truth that should have been obvious by now: "They are going
to kill me. It doesn't matter what evidence you or anyone comes
up with. They are going to murder me for a murder I didn't
commit."[6]

In October Benazir had been made a member of the PPP
central committee. Raja Anwar, a one-time Bhutto supporter
who in later years wrote thoughtfully about the PPP and his engagement with the party, has stated in no uncertain terms that
at that time "she was no more than a spare wheel to her mother."
Also, as he wrote:

Like everyone else at the time, Begum [Nusrat] Bhutto lacked
the insight to foresee her husband's fate, and therefore to plan

to circumvent it. As for the PPP, it was more a rabble than a party. Bhutto had never encouraged party democracy, or a strong local structure with solid grass-roots links. He once claimed that "I am the People's Party and they are all my creatures," a lesson that his heirs learned only too well.[7]

Anwar and others have maintained that a compromise could have been reached that might have saved Bhutto's life: he could have gone into exile, at least for a while, if he had agreed to hand over leadership of the party to one of his colleagues such as Ghulam Mustafa Jatoi, a cofounder of the PPP, who would have come to some kind of modus vivendi with the army. "However," Anwar goes on,

> the Bhutto ladies denounced all these suggestions as an army plan to deprive the Bhutto family of the leadership of the PPP and oust it from the politics of Pakistan. Would it be fair to say that in the keenness of his family's ambition, Pakistan's unique son was sacrificed? Fair or not, it is a fact that the Bhutto ladies had created such a grief-laden atmosphere around the issue that it appeared to the people of Pakistan that their only objective should be to prevent the leadership of the party from going into the hands of a non-Bhutto.[8]

Neither then nor at any other time were party elections held. The PPP had begun as a Bhutto fiefdom, and it would continue that way. Despite the stated allegiance of Benazir and her father to the parliamentary system, there was to be no democracy inside the PPP, as there is in Britain's Labour and Conservative Parties, a fact that would become increasingly galling to PPP insiders and would give the lie to Benazir's pretensions as a beacon of democracy, particularly when, in 1993, she declared herself chairperson for life. Nusrat, like her daughter, had no wish to condone dissent from other party members, and eventually the PPP would be openly referred to as the BFP, the Bhutto Family Party.

The Bhutto women's attitude was intransigent and confrontational at this point — but then, Zulfikar himself was intransigent and confrontational, and it is questionable whether he would have ever been content to compromise, much less to languish in exile, out of the limelight, in England, Switzerland, or the Arab world. If Benazir's behavior can be seen in retrospect as foolhardy, it was behavior her father would have entirely condoned.

Benazir and Nusrat had set up a PPP center in a house lent to them by a Lahore supporter: here they attempted to muster legal evidence to help Zulfikar's lawyers, led by Yayha Bakhtiar, in their battle for their client's life. They also put out a book called *Bhutto: Rumor and Reality,* a risky business since the authors or publishers of "seditious" — that is, pro-PPP — literature could be arrested and jailed. Nusrat declared a nationwide "Democracy Day" on her husband's birthday, January 5, but very little action from the Pakistani people resulted, and when people did demonstrate, the backlash from the regime was vicious.

One event that was to go down in PPP lore was the time Nusrat and Benazir decided to provoke a crisis at a cricket match in Lahore in order to demonstrate the brutality of Zia's regime. PPP supporters were stationed inside and outside Qaddafi Stadium and began shouting slogans and heckling the crowd while the police launched their predictably ferocious response. The Bhutto ladies, caught in the fracas they had instigated, both sustained injuries — particularly Nusrat, who was beaten severely about the head.

The two women would always claim that the demonstrations were spontaneous and that they just happened to be on the scene by accident: "My mother and I decide[d] to go to a cricket match to take our minds off the trial,"[9] Benazir wrote in her autobiography, insisting that the police had planned the attack on them. "The implications were enormous," she went on. "Women had never been singled out for punishment or harassment."[10] But Raja Anwar, an accomplice of theirs that day, refutes this claim, and indeed the idea that the Bhutto women would go off to watch cricket while Zulfikar's trial was under way is patently ludicrous. In any event, the propaganda was valuable to the PPP and the photographs of the bedraggled, fainting Nusrat effectively horrifying. In later years Benazir would attribute her mother's Alzheimer's disease to the beating she took that day, and this, too, was good propaganda, though medically dubious.

Throughout Z. A. Bhutto's trial, his wife and daughter were kept on tenterhooks, detained under house arrest repeatedly, then released in just as arbitrary a manner. Benazir believed that it was being done to keep them off step, unable to plan an efficient counterattack. In the intervals between detentions, Benazir toured the Bhutto homeland of Sindh, addressing legal and professional associations as well as the usual crowds, learning to project her voice powerfully as microphones had been banned by the military regime. In March, rumors began to circulate that the Lahore high court was soon to reach a guilty verdict and a death sentence for Bhutto. To quell the public expression of outrage, the regime began rounding up and detaining PPP members in the tens of thousands. These political prisoners were incarcerated in inhumane conditions, the men lashed. Benazir herself was taken into custody once again the morning of March 18; several hours later, it was revealed that Z. A. Bhutto had indeed been found guilty of murder and sentenced to death.

The fruitless appeal process ground out over the course of the next year, during which time the unhappy Zulfikar languished in increasing deprivation and discomfort. He was emaciated, and his gums became severely infected. Benazir visited him on the rare occasions that this was allowed, bringing him gifts of books and bottles of his favorite Shalimar cologne, but she, too, was frequently held in custody, unable to see him. Appeals for clemency poured in from world leaders, including Leonid Brezhnev, Indira Gandhi, James Callaghan, Muammar Qaddafi, Anwar Sadat, and even, after much hesitation, US president Jimmy Carter. Ill as he was, Zulfikar did not sit idle: he prepared his own legal appeal, speaking before the court for four days without notes, and managed to smuggle a manuscript out of his cell giving his view of the conspiracy against him, destined for a columnist at the *Financial Times*.

Benazir acted as his amanuensis, holing up with his legal team to type out his rejoinder to the charges, later circulated in mimeograph under the title of *If I Am Assassinated*. She was supported by her friends Yasmin Niazi, Amina Piracha, and Victoria Schofield, who had succeeded her as president of the Oxford Union and had now come over from England to stand at her side. Nusrat began setting up people's action committees to agitate locally against the regime, with volunteers committing civil disobedience and courting arrest. On September 15, 1978, the day before Zia ul-Haq proclaimed himself Pakistan's president, the first of these demonstrations occurred in the city of Rawalpindi, where Bhutto was being held in prison. The agitation spread to other cities, and two members of the action committees even set themselves on fire. Benazir and Nusrat toured the country, giving speeches and calling for a countrywide day of protest.

Inevitably, every effort to save Bhutto failed. Zia could not risk keeping him alive, even in exile. While Bhutto had been an authoritarian, strong-arm leader who, for all his populist rhetoric, had done very little for Pakistan's common man, he symbolized something much greater than himself: hope for the impoverished Pakistani Everyman. He may not have improved life for Pakistan's poor, but at least he had, unlike nearly all his predecessors, acknowledged their needs and their humanity. There has always been a religious element in Pakistani politics, enhanced by the fact that so many political figures came from great *wadero* families. The subcontinent is rich with the tombs of Muslim "saints," or *shaikhs;* like Christian saints, the *shaikhs* serve as intermediaries between the higher power and the people, and local cults grew up around their tombs with tales of miracles performed by the defunct *shaikhs.*[11] Descendants of the *shaikhs* are known as *pirs,* and their feudal authority is enhanced by the aura of sanctity around the family. The Bhuttos of Larkana were a particularly notable *pir* family, and they augmented their position by assiduous attention to their religious duties as guardians of the local cult. The family's status as *pirs* permeated the culture of the PPP, of which other prominent *pirs* were also founding members. Observers have remarked that PPP rallies resembled revival meetings, with supporters chanting slogans in a state of apparently religious rapture.

The question of just how sincere the nominally secular Bhuttos' participation in these cults was is unanswerable. There can be no doubt that they manipulated the people's credulity to their advantage, following Machiavelli's time-honored advice. The high-living Zulfikar's religious pretensions seem particularly dubious. But Benazir, who was one day to outdo even her father in high living, seems to have had some genuine, if unorthodox, religious belief, mixed up with superstition — rather in the manner of a believing Christian who consults astrologers. She strewed her conversation with the phrase "*inshallah*" and claimed to believe the Koran favored the equality of the sexes. In a 2002 interview in the *Guardian* she would affirm her belief in Sufism, the mystical branch of Islam, and — rather astoundingly, considering she was airing these views in a British publication — that supernatural powers, ineffable but genuine, attended the Bhutto family. "I find that whenever I am in power, or my father was in power," she asserted, "somehow good things happen. The economy picks up, we have good rains, water comes, people have crops. I think the reason this happens is that we want to give love and we receive love."[12]

Can this be seen as the beginning of a sort of mania, a genuine belief that her family enjoyed divine status? In any case, it is certainly an indication of a legacy Benazir carried into her political life: the extreme paternalism of her culture, one that could not be washed away with eight years of education in the democratic West. There are good and bad aspects of this paternalism. On the one hand, families like the Bhuttos felt, or at any rate were compelled to say they felt, responsibility toward "their" people, of a sort that few American or British politicians still feel. On the other, the very concept of paternalism is antidemocratic. A populist politician who is also a feudal lord is a contradiction in terms; one who is a demigod, of whatever political stripe, can hardly be said to be a democrat at all. The Bhutto family, of course, is not the only Asian dynasty that has exploited its local belief system to invest itself with a divine aura. At this same time, the 1970s, Indian prime minister Indira Gandhi was employing iconography that implicitly deified her family; in Syria today, the same process is being carried on by the Assads as they struggle to maintain their tenuous hold on an unraveling country.

What is certain is that after his execution at Rawalpindi on April 4, 1979, Z. A. Bhutto became a more obvious object of religious reverence. He was now a martyr, a *shaheed,* and as such a powerful weapon in the hands of his successors in the PPP, as Benazir, more than anyone, knew. Always aware of the magical aura of the *shaheed,* she played on this identity for the rest of her career, making sure that her father's image was always displayed somewhere in the vicinity of her own, endowing hers with its sympathetic magic. Zia, too, understood the magic, and feared it; in the 1980s he razed Rawalpindi Jail to the ground lest the building become a potent symbol, a *shaheed*'s shrine.

With this in mind, fearing riots, Zia had arranged to have Bhutto executed before dawn. He had detained Nusrat and Benazir in a police camp several miles away. None of Bhutto's nearest and dearest was with him when he died, and there is even some mystery about how the execution was enacted; he was supposed to be hung—a gallows had been erected—but a servant who helped to bury him insisted that his neck had not been broken. His body was transferred by air to the family burial ground of Garhi Khuda Bakhsh at Larkana. His first, "feudal" wife, Amir Begum, was brought from the family compound to join relatives at the graveside as he was lowered into the ground; Nusrat and Benazir were absent, as of course were Zulfikar's other children.

Did Zia and the military act independently when they deposed Bhutto and declared martial law, or was Mustafa Khar correct when he suspected Zia of being manipulated by "bigger powers"? Specifically, was the CIA involved? Many observers have pointed out that the chain of events in Pakistan in 1977 was markedly similar to the CIA-backed ouster of Salvador Allende in Chile four years earlier. Ramsey Clark announced his conclusions in a speech at Stanford University: "I don't believe in conspiracy theories in general, but the similarities in the staging of riots in Chile . . . and in Pakistan are just too close."[13] He pointed out that "Bhutto was removed from power in Pakistan on 5 July, after the usual party on the 4th at the US embassy at Islamabad, with US approval, if not more, by General Zia ul-Haq. Bhutto was falsely accused and brutalized for months during proceedings that corrupted the judiciary of Pakistan before being murdered, then hanged."[14] Clark might also have pointed out that the most damaging witness for the prosecution was spirited away to safety in the United States after the trial. "As

Americans," Clark insisted, "we must ask ourselves this: is it possible that a rational military leader under the circumstances in Pakistan could have overthrown a constitutional government, without at least the tacit approval of the United States?"[15]

A reasonable question, hard to answer in the negative. Pakistan's leaders have always been heavily dependent on US good will and munificence, and Zia, in particular, would prove a master at manipulating the CIA, the White House, the State Department, and the Pentagon. If indeed the CIA was involved in Bhutto's downfall, it could have been his intransigence on the subject of the Pakistani bomb that did for him: Bhutto insisted that at a private meeting in 1976, Kissinger had threatened to make "a horrible example" of him if he persisted in his nuclear ambitions. Bhutto himself believed that the CIA had been responsible for his fall, as did Benazir. But she knew the value of a good working relationship with the United States and would not play the blame game too loudly.

Now President of Pakistan, and with Bhutto finally gone, Zia ul-Haq set about his Islamization program in earnest. With no political party of his own, he created, along with his cronies the Sharif brothers (Nawaz and Shahbaz), the new Pakistan Muslim League. The most infamous of his fundamentalist edicts were the so-called Hudood Ordinances of 1979. These were centered on *zina* — laws concerning sexual intercourse between a man and woman who were not married. The ordinances regulated legal positions on adultery, prostitution, and rape. According to these new laws, a woman who had been raped could and often would be prosecuted for adultery. Punishments included public flogging, amputation, and, in some cases, stoning to death. Thankfully, Pakistani doctors refused to perform the amputations, so this punishment at least found few victims.

The usual way to describe such doings is "medieval," but this is not really fair, for during the Middle Ages Islam was surprisingly tolerant: the great medieval Muslim kingdoms of Andalusia and Sicily were known for their ecumenical spirit, and thrived because of it. The intolerant and retrograde species of Islam enforced by Zia was more typical of Wahhabism, the puritanical sect that arose during the eighteenth century in what is now Saudi Arabia. It is probable that the intensification of Zia's program was prompted not merely by his personal piety, although that was genuine enough, but by the fall of the shah of Iran in 1979. The shah, a Westernized secularist like Bhutto, had failed to understand the force of religious fervor in Iranian life, and he had paid the price. Zia was not going to give the Pakistani zealots an opportunity to call their leader an infidel.

General Zia ul-Haq, the Uriah Heep of Pakistani politics, devoid of charisma or apparent brilliance, turned out to be far more adept than the glittering Z. A. Bhutto at manipulating international opinion and coaxing the Americans to open their coffers. The many people who had accepted his humility at face value might have remembered that in fact he was no dummy, having received a BA in economics with the highest marks in his college at the University of Delhi. Granted, an enormous gift fell into his lap: the Soviet invasion of Afghanistan in 1979. But he was to prove masterful at maximizing its benefits.

Jimmy Carter, appalled by the human rights violations of Zia's Islamization measures and deeply concerned about the Pakistani nuclear program, had cut back the military aid that had been flowing from America to Pakistan for so long, and forces within the US Senate had been attempting to rein in Pakistani nuclear ambitions with laws that would link aid to compliance with international regulations. The 1976 Symington Amendment to the 1961 Foreign Assistance Act banned economic and military assistance to countries that did not comply with International Atomic Energy Agency regulations and inspections; a further amendment, sponsored in 1977 by John Glenn, laid out sanctions against countries buying or selling nuclear reprocessing technology. Citing this legislation, Carter announced that there would be no further aid to Pakistan. The execution of Z. A. Bhutto and the imprisonment of his wife and daughter made the American president even more reluctant to subsidize this military dictator.

But even before the Soviet invasion Zia had begun playing

on the susceptibilities of anticommunist hard-liners in the Pentagon, trying to interest them in the Muslim jihad against godless communists and their Soviet sponsors in Afghanistan. And the anticommunist line, once again, proved ultimately persuasive. As Husain Haqqani, a one-time Pakistani ambassador to the United States, points out, "For years the conventional narrative about the war in Afghanistan has revolved around the Soviet invasion in December 1979. But Carter signed the first authorization 'to help the Mujahideen covertly' on July 3, 1979, almost six months before the Soviets invaded Afghanistan."[1] The actual invasion, which took place five months later, made it very difficult for the Carter administration to justify blocking military aid to Pakistan on the grounds of its nuclear ambitions. Pakistan was now a "front-line country," as Zia reminded the Americans at every opportunity, in the holy war against communism. Afghanistan, with a little American backing, could become the Soviet Vietnam.

So nuclear worries were put on the back burner in Washington, and Carter made an offer to Pakistan's military dictator: $400 million in economic and military aid, to be delivered over two years. Zia dismissed this as "peanuts," surely a calculated insult to Carter, the former peanut farmer. He could afford to hold out for more: election season was under way in the United States, and things were looking very bad for Carter, with the staunch anticommunist Ronald Reagan poised in the wings, almost certain to take office after the 1980 election. And Zia didn't have long to wait: with the accession of Reagan, who chose the hawkish Alexander Haig as his secretary of state and the equally avid anti-Soviet William Casey as CIA director, the dollars began flowing fast. Zia blandly informed the new administration that the Pakistanis had no intention of building a bomb, and Reagan elected to believe him. In June 1981 the State Department announced six years' exemption for Pakistan from the Symington Amendment, and a $3.2 billion military and

economic aid program for the country's sponsorship of the mujahideen's crusade against the Soviets, masterminded by Pakistan's ISI — an agency that would grow exponentially under Zia
until, like the American CIA, it assumed a life of its own, independent of both government and military. There would be no
hang-ups like the Symington and Glenn Amendments to slow
the works. Zia sweetened the deal for the Americans by dangling before them the prospect of American military bases in
Pakistan. Anti-Soviet hard-liners in the United States painted
the conflict in Afghanistan in the simplistic colors of a John
Wayne cowboys-and-Indians movie, the plucky mujahideen pit-
ted against the Soviet behemoth.[2]

Still, there were those who objected to Zia's human rights record, his execution of his predecessor, his obvious lies about Pakistani nuclear ambitions. For these naysayers there was crafted
in 1985 another amendment to the Foreign Assistance Act, this
one specifically aimed at Pakistan. The Pressler Amendment allowed the aid to keep flowing as long as the American president
certified each year that "Pakistan does not possess a nuclear explosive device and that the proposed United States assistance
program will reduce significantly the risk that Pakistan will possess a nuclear explosive device." With only the ideologue Reagan's word required to keep the largesse flowing, and with the
Saudis matching American contributions dollar for dollar, Zia
was in the catbird seat.

In the meantime, Nusrat and Benazir Bhutto were still perceived as a threat, and still harassed without mercy. They spent
half of the year after Zulfikar's death under "protective custody"
at al-Murtaza, the beginning of a cat-and-mouse game Zia would
play with the Bhutto women for the next decade. House arrest
was capriciously enforced and lifted throughout 1980 and the
early part of 1981. But Nusrat and Benazir, not to be intimidated,
continued their political activities, taking a prominent role in

forming a broad coalition of resistance to Zia's rule, the Movement for the Restoration of Democracy (MRD). This was a partnership among eleven parties of widely different political persuasions, including the PPP, the Awami National Party, the Islamist Jamiat-ul-Ulema-e-Islam, the leftist Mazdoor Kissan Party, and the moderate Tehrik-e-Istiqlal. It was to be a nonviolent movement of protest in the Gandhian tradition. In this case, politics did indeed make strange bedfellows: the new alliance was even joined by some components of the PNA, the coalition that had opposed Z. A. Bhutto in 1977, thus setting the military coup in motion. In spite of much mutual suspicion (Benazir, in particular, was loath to admit her father's enemies into the sacred precincts of 70 Clifton), the uneasy partners signed the MRD charter on February 6, 1981, and sent out a press release. Students, professors, lawyers, and doctors across the nation took to the streets, and Zia closed down universities and banned gatherings of more than five people. The MRD set the date of March 23 for a nationwide day of strikes and demonstrations. But before that, there was a major setback for Benazir and for the PPP cause.

In Europe, the Bhutto brothers, Murtaza and Shah Nawaz, had taken up the fight in their own way. During their father's imprisonment and trial they had mounted an international campaign called the "Save Bhutto Committee," but aside from a few staunch allies — Yasir Arafat, Hafiz al-Assad, Muammar Qaddafi, France's Valéry Giscard d'Estaing — they had not managed to mobilize sufficient international support for direct intervention. This lack of active support from foreign governments had persuaded the brothers that armed resistance was the answer. In London they had joined forces with Mustafa Khar, now in exile, and began to put together an armed force, an organization that could oppose Zia's regime in a militant manner. Khar's wife recalled the era:

Mir [Murtaza] was a novice, but he learned fast. Younger brother Shah Nawaz exhibited the idealistic, faraway gaze of the revolutionary. They established a sort of headquarters of disgruntled Pakistanis in our flat, and plotted Zia's overthrow . . . Our drawing room was converted into a firing range. Mir set up a target at one end of the room and practiced his marksmanship with an air gun. I was not terribly impressed; he seemed to be just a spirited youngster, playing at terror . . . For his part, Shah Nawaz looked more like a suave terrorist, but his soft eyes gave him away. He did not seem to be able to force a steely-cold look into them.[3]

These activities did not end after Bhutto's execution: on the contrary, the boys had expanded their operations. In 1979 Syrian president Hafiz al-Assad had offered them asylum in Damascus, and there they had set up operations for the "People's Liberation Army," an armed guerrilla movement that they hoped would eventually oust Zia's military government. Later that same year they relocated to Kabul, where they established a terrorist organization they dubbed al-Zulfikar, the Sword. The Palestine Liberation Army provided them with arms, delivered to them in Kabul by Syrian aircraft, but declined to take part in any actual military activities.

Observers at the time remembered Mir Murtaza and Shah Nawaz as being impossibly romantic. Murtaza modeled himself on his heroes Mao and Che, and wrote overheated letters to his girlfriend of the period, a beautiful older woman married to an imprisoned Greek general. "I am sure of success," one of them reads. "Because the people are with us; the dynamics of history are with us . . . Don't worry about me, my destiny will be decided through the barrel of a gun."[4] The boys followed Che, too, in their personal indulgences. They were well funded by al-Zulfikar's international allies, and the revenue from the Bhutto family lands, still substantial despite Z. A. Bhutto's land reforms, was generous. Like their father, they favored Turnbull & Asser shirts and silk suits; Murtaza had a liking for Geoffrey Beene cologne. The women who were seen with them were similarly elegant and well-heeled.

In 1981 Murtaza and Shah Nawaz married two Afghani sisters, Fowzia and Raehana Fasihudin, the daughters of a senior official in the Afghan Ministry of Foreign Affairs. Murtaza and Fowzia's daughter, Fatima, who was born in 1982, would grow up to become one of her aunt Benazir's most vocal and devastating critics; she has also been her father's most passionate apologist, and her 2010 book *Songs of Blood and Sword,* a fascinating tale written by a brilliant woman, nevertheless bears a startling resemblance to Benazir's *Daughter of Destiny* in its author's inability to look at her adored father with any balance.

Others have been able to provide the necessary distance, however. Raja Anwar, at that time a close associate of the brothers, remembers Mir Murtaza and Shah Nawaz's first meeting with their troops:

> Not only was [Murtaza] wearing an "awami" suit, a long kurta and shalwar, in the image of his father, but like him, he had the sleeves unbuttoned. There was only one sofa in the room, which could seat only him. To hammer home his revolutionary credentials, he had a Kalashnikov resting against his left forearm ... Shah Nawaz, Murtaza's younger brother, sported an Arab keffiyeh. He was wearing army fatigues, with a string of hand-grenades hanging from his belt and a dagger hugging his right thigh. An extra magazine had been secured to his Kalashnikov with the help of scotch tape. This was something he had seen PLO fighters do.[5]

Al-Zulfikar's early recruits tended to be idealistic young men like the Bhutto brothers themselves. Some of them were killed during the group's early incursions across the border into Pakistan. As time went on, these were replaced with a more ruthless and battle-hardened group. One especially scary character was the twenty-five-year-old Salamullah Tipu, a militant member of the PPP's student wing, who had killed a pro-Zia student at the University of Karachi. It was he who pulled off what was to be al-Zulfikar's most "successful"—if that is the correct word—act: the hijacking, on March 2, 1981 (the very moment that the MRD was desperately trying to mobilize support) of a Pakistan International Airways flight. Tipu, along with two other young men, hijacked the passenger flight originally bound for Peshawar, rerouting it to Kabul, where it sat on the tarmac for seven days, its passengers held prisoner at gunpoint while al-Zulfikar demanded the release of fifty-five political prisoners currently being held in Pakistani jails. One passenger was shot dead, a diplomat named Tariq Rahim who, ironically enough, had been a close associate and aide-de-camp of Z. A. Bhutto. After the plane had sat for a week on the ground in Kabul, during which time Murtaza and the ISI chief Dr. Nasibullah negotiated, it was agreed that the political prisoners would be released. The PIA plane then proceeded to Damascus. The crisis in its entirety lasted thirteen days.

Just who was responsible for this move has been a source of disagreement for some time. Fatima Bhutto claims that her father had rejected Tipu's idea of a hijacking in no uncertain terms, and that once the deed was done, he pleaded with Tipu to release the prisoners. Peter Galbraith, who had access to US government intelligence, gives it as his opinion that "the hijacking occurred independently, the hijackers declared themselves to be al-Zulfikar, and then the [Bhutto] boys idiotically went to the airport and embraced them."[6] But other accounts, including Raja Anwar's authoritative insider account of al-Zulfikar, have indicated that Murtaza was behind the hijacking.

Benazir, needless to say, was horrified: the hijacking garnered all the attention al-Zulfikar had hoped for and then some, but the only international PR it gained for the Bhutto cause and that of the PPP was, as far as she could see, of the worst possible kind. The Bhuttos and the PPP were supposed to be beacons for democracy, not murderous terrorists, but the government was putting about the idea that al-Zulfikar was the armed branch of the PPP and that Benazir and her mother had approved the hijacking, as well as al-Zulfikar's other violent actions. The hijacking rendered Benazir's own position infinitely more dangerous; Zia, who now felt justified in the use of force, rounded up thousands of political enemies — specifically MRD members — in a nationwide witch hunt, and Benazir herself was one of the first to be arrested, the police tracking her down on March 7 at the home of friends.

She was initially held in the Karachi Central Jail, then taken by plane to solitary confinement in the Sukkur Central Jail, isolated in the deserts of central Sindh, where she spent five months of intense discomfort. Temperatures in her cell reached as high as 120 degrees; dust swirled through it; insects infested it. She developed a severe mastoid infection; soon the clicking in her ear became constant and she began to lose her hearing. Her hair fell out in clumps and her eyesight began to fail. Allowed neither visitors nor newspapers, without any reliable source of information, she began to fear that the prison authorities intended to kill her, or to torture her in order to extract a confession of involvement in the hijacking. Suffering from a gynecological disorder as well as her other ailments, she lost her appetite and developed anorexia.

Nusrat, who had been jailed in Karachi while Benazir was at Sukkur, was released in July when she was diagnosed with cancer, and allowed to go to Europe for medical treatment. A month later, Benazir was transferred to Karachi and put into her mother's former cell, where she stayed until being released to house arrest in December. She was to remain under house arrest, first at al-Murtaza and then at 70 Clifton, for the next two years.

Benazir's actions were closely monitored by the regime and the intelligence services. A draconian new martial law had made it a capital offense to do anything "liable to cause insecurity, fear or despondency among the public." The MRD, whose actions Benazir was closely following from house arrest and with which she was once again in illicit communication, was calling for agitation. Benazir issued a public statement to the nation, in the name of her now-absent mother, that fueled a furious uprising throughout Sindh in the summer of 1983, a rebellion subsequently crushed by the Pakistani military. Undaunted, she continued her resistance to the illegitimate regime from confinement at 70 Clifton. This heroic commitment to the cause of democracy in spite of her horrific experiences in the Sukkur Central Jail impressed international observers — even in Washington, where Zia's star was still very much in the ascendant.

B HUTTO, LIKE HER foe Zia, was discovering that American support was all-important to her political career, if not her very survival. Her father had designed her trajectory so that she might acquire the right connections as well as the right education, and these efforts now began to pay off, particularly in the person of Peter Galbraith, who had risen steadily in the Washington establishment since his years at Harvard and Oxford.

Galbraith had received a law degree from Georgetown after leaving Oxford, and in 1979 he took a staff job on the Senate Foreign Relations Committee, where he handled Near Eastern and South Asian affairs. He had maintained contact with Benazir and now observed her situation with concern. In Washington he and his mentor, Senator Claiborne Pell, persistently reminded their colleagues of the Bhutto women's plight at the hands of the American client Zia, and lobbied on their behalf with various influential senators and congressmen. Beginning in 1981 Galbraith sought meetings with Benazir herself, but this possibility was denied by Pakistan's military authorities. It was also most strenuously discouraged by the Reagan administration, which had ruled that no US government personnel were allowed to have contact with any member of the Bhutto family: Zia was too important to Reagan's grand plan in Afghanistan.

Galbraith and Nusrat Bhutto flouted this injunction when they met in Pakistan that year: Nusrat chose one of the most public meeting spots she could think of, the Karachi Boat Club, as a gesture of defiance.

Zia's 1982 visit to Washington was in most aspects a love-fest: as Reagan wrote in his diary, "We got along fine. He's a good man (cavalry). Gave me his word they were not building an atomic or nuclear bomb. He's dedicated to helping the Afghans and stopping the Soviets."[1] But Pell and Galbraith managed to remind the members of the Senate Foreign Relations Committee who met with Zia that the general was not such a good man after all. Pell specifically brought up Zia's treatment of the Bhutto women and Zia defended his actions, claiming that in fact Benazir lived in comfort and had easy access to the telephone: "Senator, she lives in a better house than any of you senators. She can use the phone, and friends can visit her." "Immediately then I went out and called," Galbraith comments, "and of course they wouldn't let me speak to her."[2]

Galbraith admits to having finagled a deal that would enable him to meet with Benazir. The Reagan administration was keen to appoint Deane Hinton as US ambassador to Pakistan, but he had been a longtime CIA officer and the Senate hearing process promised to drag out for a long time and to be embarrassing for all parties. Galbraith negotiated a quid pro quo whereby Hinton's confirmation would be pushed through the Senate without a hearing if, once he was ensconced in Islamabad, Hinton would help arrange a meeting between Galbraith and Benazir. Hinton duly departed for Pakistan in November 1983. Galbraith arrived there on January 9, 1984, but to his surprise he discovered that Benazir had just been put on a plane, headed for Europe and medical treatment. Zia's administration had decided to cut its losses and not risk further embarrassment over its treatment of the Bhutto ladies; besides, as Galbraith

points out, if she had died, either of illness or in mysterious circumstances on the operating table, Zia's aid package might have
been in real trouble. The American's decisive intervention had
possibly saved Benazir's life.

In London she was reunited with her family at an aunt's
Knightsbridge flat. She underwent microscopic surgery on her
mastoid at the end of the month and could then, in theory, go
back to resume her struggle in Pakistan. According to her autobiography, she decided to stay in London instead because she
would be required to have another operation in nine to twelve
months' time. She may perhaps have felt some need to defend
her decision to leave Pakistan after having doggedly hung on
there for so long, but no excuse is necessary: she turned out to
be far more effective leading the opposition to Zia from London, where she was free to publish, communicate, and publicize her cause, than from Karachi, where her every move was
monitored.

Bhutto swung into action in characteristically energetic
style, drawing international attention to Zia's horrendous human rights abuses and to the plight of the forty thousand political prisoners languishing in Pakistan's miserable jails. A few days
after her arrival in London she met with Galbraith, en route to
Washington after his trip to the subcontinent. He stressed the
importance of American backing for the message she was trying to get across, and for her future political career if she was
to have one. Reagan and the Afghanistan hawks would have
preferred to ignore Benazir and the Bhutto family entirely, but
other lawmakers were concerned with Zia's human rights record and might be eager to talk to her. "You need to come to the
United States," Galbraith urged Benazir, "because basically the
Reagan administration thinks you are a pro-communist sympa-
thizer against the U.S. cause in Afghanistan, a radical, and they
want to have this alliance with Pakistan. You need to be able to

persuade them that you'll be just as good for them as Zia, except that you'll have more popular support."³ He also tried to help her hone her oratorical style. "She was so intense. And so I'd say, slow down. Speak slowly. Just have one or two points."⁴

She followed Galbraith's sage advice closely, making a trip to the United States later that year. In New York she went right to the top of the media heap, setting up a meeting with *Time* magazine editor Walter Isaacson, another Harvard buddy. In Washington, Galbraith put her up at his apartment on Capitol Hill, and while Reagan's White House made no overtures, Galbraith introduced her to as many influential people as he could, including Senators Pell, Charles Mathias, Ed Zorinsky, Alan Cranston, Paul Tsongas, Edward Kennedy, and Charles Percy, and Congressman Stephen Solarz. He also introduced her to a lawyer named Mark Siegel, who became her unofficial American lobbyist during these years and her official one after she came to power. From this time on, Siegel would be a powerful force in "packaging" Benazir for an American audience. Later, he would collaborate with her on her posthumously published 2008 book *Reconciliation: Islam, Democracy and the West,* and he would update her autobiography after her death, adding a final chapter and epilogue. He also produced a staggeringly one-sided biopic about her three years after her death, possibly with an eye to the future political career of her son, Bilawal.

In London Benazir took a flat at the Barbican Estate, a brutalist apartment block, and there, in relative safety, finally began to regain not only her health but also her once-ebullient personality. Catherine Drucker, her Oxford friend recalls the era:

> Benazir used to organize dinners there. I was always impressed by how well she cooked, for a person who always lived with servants.
>
> When she came out of arrest, she was in a mildly trauma-

tized state, jumping at sudden noise and worrying about who might be spying on her. I think she chose to live at the Barbican, that great ugly place, for its good security. But I can remember having fun with her in those days, going to grand teas at the Savoy, shopping for boots, going to movies. One was Hanif Kureishi's *My Beautiful Laundrette*.[5]

The Barbican flat quickly became the headquarters of PPP members in exile, staffed by Pakistani volunteers: the group continued its campaign to publicize the atrocities committed by the Zia regime and the mistreatment — and occasional execution — of its political prisoners. It also became the center of an inevitable power struggle within the PPP, "an undeclared battle for party leadership," in Benazir's words.[6] She had been confirmed as acting chairperson of the party by the central executive committee upon her arrival in England, but many of the party's elder statesmen were not at all sure they approved of this choice. Some objected to her inexperience; the not insignificant Marxist contingent worried that she was not sufficiently committed to socialist principles; most of all, party stalwarts worried that with the accession of Z. A. Bhutto's daughter to the top position, the party would become a Bhutto family fiefdom — a fear that would prove only too well founded. The failure, then and later, to hold intraparty elections for the leadership of the PPP would ensure that the Bhutto family, with its brand-name appeal and beyond-the-grave blessing from its own personal *shaheed,* would maintain control.

Zia, under pressure from his sponsors in the United States, decreed that elections would be held in March 1985, but before that date he decided to stage a referendum: "Whether the people of Pakistan endorse the process initiated by General Mohammed Zia ul-Haq, the President of Pakistan, for bringing the laws of Holy Quran and Sunnah of the Holy Prophet (Peace Be

Upon Him)." As Benazir, who was watching the proceedings from Britain, wondered, how could it lose? "A 'no' vote was tantamount to voting against Islam."[7] And a "yes" vote, Zia had announced, would confirm his "election" as president for the next five years. To help ensure that the vote would go his way, he said that campaigning for a "no" vote would be punishable by heavy fines and prison sentences, and also that the army would do the vote counting and that the results would not be liable to challenge by the courts.

From London, the PPP in exile urged voters to boycott the vote, the only possible approach they could take, and on referendum day only 10 percent of eligible voters went to the polls. Zia then announced elections for February, which the PPP again advised voters to boycott. They were less successful this time, perhaps because Zia now made boycotting, too, a crime punishable by imprisonment. But Bhutto could not have been dissatisfied with the outcome of the vote: it demonstrated that the PPP was still the strongest party in the country, despite having been officially outlawed. Zia tried to minimize the damage by making amendments to the constitution, reconfirming his presidency for five years. Under American pressure (the land of the free shouldn't be seen funding a military dictator) he agreed to be sworn in as a civilian rather than a military president. But as Bhutto later pointed out, "Zia was still Army Chief-of-Staff. And dressing occasionally in a long tunic instead of a uniform did not change his stripes."[8]

Bhutto returned to America in April, delivering a lecture at Harvard and another at the Council on Foreign Relations. Then she went on to Strasbourg, where she addressed the European Parliament. Her final stop was in Cannes in the south of France, where there was to be a family reunion, the first meeting of the four Bhutto siblings since their father's death. Shah Nawaz had been living in nearby Nice with his wife, Raehana, and their little daughter, Sassi. Sanam arrived from London, and Nusrat from Geneva, where she had been living in exile. Murtaza came from Damascus with his wife, Fowzia, Raehana's sister, and their daughter, Fatima. Fatima and Sassi were both three years old.

The family spent several festive days together, although it was clear that Shah and Raehana's marriage was not a happy one. On the night of July 17 there was a celebratory barbecue on the beach at La Napoule, after which Shah and Murtaza got into separate cars to drive the relatives home. By the time the two brothers and their wives had reconvened at Shah's place, it was apparent that Shah and Raehana had quarreled; Murtaza intervened and was kicked out of the apartment by Raehana. Eventually things seemed to be settling down, with Raehana and Sassi in the bedroom getting ready to sleep. But the following afternoon, Raehana came to find Murtaza at his mother's flat; something was the matter with Shah, she said. Stopping to call the police, Murtaza hurried back with Raehana to find Shah's body facedown on the living room floor. He had been poisoned with the little vial of toxin he and his brother both kept in case they were taken by enemies. Poisoned at whose hand, no one knew.

The truth about Shah's death was never discovered. He might have killed himself—his marriage was on the rocks and he had been depressed—but no one in the Bhutto family considered it a possibility. Nor would they be likely to, for in Muslim societies suicide carries a stigma. Fowzia, Murtaza's wife, subscribed to the suicide theory, saying that the Bhutto family was too proud to admit that such a thing was possible. However, there was no suicide note, and the timing would have been very odd for a suicide. Newspapers in Pakistan speculated that Shah had died of drug and alcohol abuse. Murtaza believed that Zia's regime, or the ISI and CIA, had engineered a hit, and it is true that the Bhutto brothers constituted a perpetual threat to the current government. Shah and Murtaza had garnered plenty of other enemies, too, during their years at the helm of al-Zulfikar, for they had hardly stopped their terrorist activities after the hijacking; their next target, in fact, had been the chief justice who had sentenced Z. A. Bhutto to death, and though al-Zulfikar operatives missed him when they opened fire on his car, they had inadvertently succeeded in killing a friend who was with him at the time. The Bhutto brothers had made enemies within al-Zulfikar, too, for they ruled high-handedly and were extremely careless with the lives of their followers.

Fatima Bhutto has expressed her own suspicion that Raehana had something to do with her husband's death. There was no evidence that Raehana had played an active role, but neither can there be any doubt that her behavior at the time was strange. It turned out that Shah had not died instantaneously, and his wife had certainly taken her time before seeking help. "In Raehana's police testimony," Fatima writes, "there is a suggestion that she did not help Shah as he lay dying, but a clear assertion that she did not kill him."[9] The French police, too, thought Raehana's behavior suspicious, and she was detained and temporarily imprisoned in Nice before being released for lack of evidence.

According to Peter Galbraith, Benazir's personal belief was that Raehana had killed her brother. "Boys with toys," Galbraith said — "they had poisons that were provided by the Syrian secret services . . . That's what Benazir thought."[10] In any case, Benazir and Murtaza filed a case against Raehana in France, citing the Good Samaritan laws. By this time Raehana was in California with her family; in France, to which she did not return, she was convicted in absentia for not coming to the aid of a dying man. Benazir speculated openly, and pointedly, about how she had obtained a US visa.

Shah's death was a sad one, but not terribly surprising considering his life path. Benazir, with her heightened sense of her family's quasi-divine status and her unorthodox interpretation of Islam, presented it as Sophoclean tragedy, the immutable workings of Destiny:

> Many in Pakistan have come to believe that the victimization of the Bhutto family and our supporters was the Karbala of our generation. The father was not spared. The mother was not spared. The brothers were not spared. The daughter was not spared. The band of followers were not spared. Yet, like the followers of the Prophet's grandson, our resolve never faltered.[11]

One might dismiss this as pure rhetoric, a cynical manipulation of Pakistani religious sensibilities, but it was written for a Western audience, and with a straight face. Can she really have taken herself and her all-too-human family this seriously? If so, what does it say about her ability to lead in a genuinely democratic spirit?

Five days after burying her brother, and now back in Karachi, Bhutto was arrested again, charged with visiting "terrorists" in "sensitive" areas. The regime must have been made nervous by the large crowds of supporters she had attracted since her arrival in the country, and she was now issued a ninety-day detention order at 70 Clifton, temporarily deemed a sub-jail.

8

THE LIFTING OF martial law on December 30, 1985, was effected with fanfare, but as Bhutto noted, the change of government was mostly cosmetic: Zia was still president and army chief of staff, despite his civilian uniform. He had also pushed through a constitutional amendment that indemnified the regime not only for actions taken under martial law but also for actions that might yet be taken under the remaining months of martial law. Bhutto had returned to Europe after her spell of detention, but she now began to consider a permanent return to Pakistan. If she was arrested on arrival, it would prove the hollowness of Zia's promises; if not, she could begin serious political agitation, organizing mass demonstrations to pressure Zia into holding elections.

She was nervous about returning, and she had every reason to be. She was regularly receiving threats on her life, with allies who were in touch with the military warning her that she might well be assassinated on her return. She also feared the CIA, for Zia was still very much Washington's man. She remembered the fate of Benigno Aquino, gunned down on his arrival at Manila airport two years previously, after three years of exile. It was Corazon Aquino, the feisty woman who had taken on her family's mantle of leadership against a hated dictator, with whom Bhutto wished to be identified, not the ill-fated Benigno. Preparing for a return to the struggle, she began a tour for the purpose of placating powers both worldly and supernatural: to Washington; to Mecca, where she performed the Muslim *Umrah;* to the Soviet Union, so as not to be accused by leftist PPP members of leaning too far toward the United States; and back to London, where she was greeted by hosts of reporters wanting to know more about her announced departure for Pakistan on April 10. By now she had become a master of Western-style PR, and as she noted with some satisfaction, the press enjoyed seeing her political challenge as "a dramatic and poignant confrontation between a young woman and a military dictator, a modern and feminist version of David and Goliath."[1]

After eight years of autocratic theocracy, pro-democracy Pakistanis were desperate for a change, and when Bhutto arrived at Lahore they turned out to greet her in numbers that were unprecedented even in that city's volatile history. She never forgot the feeling and would spend the rest of her life trying to regain it:

There are moments in life which are not possible to describe [Bhutto wrote in her autobiography]. My return to Lahore was one of them. The sea of humanity lining the roads, jammed on balconies and roofs, wedged in trees and on lampposts, walking alongside the truck and stretching back across the fields, was more like an ocean. The eight-mile drive from the airport to the Minar-i-Pakistan in Iqbal Park usually takes fifteen minutes. On the unbelievable day of April 10, 1986, it took us ten hours. The figure of one million people at the airport grew to two million, then three million by the time we reached the Minar-i-Pakistan.

Hundreds of colored balloons soared into the sky as the airport gates opened. Rose petals, not tear gas, filled the air, showering onto the truck until they rose above my ankles. Garlands of flowers flew through the air. I saw a girl whose father had been hanged and threw a garland to her. More gar-

lands were thrown onto the truck, as were hundreds of hand-
made *dupattas* and shawls. I put one *dupatta* after another on
my head and slung others on my shoulder.[2]

Later in life, Benazir would be accused of having become addicted to power. It might be more correct to say that she became
addicted to adulation, and if so, this return to Pakistan was a
key moment in the process. It is difficult for Westerners to comprehend the sheer magnitude of public display and participation that marks the subcontinental political process: the surging
crowds, the hysterical chanting and shouting, the dancing, the
swaying, the jumping on cars. Many of us have seen footage of
Mahatma Gandhi's famous salt marches, an impressive enough
sight; since that time, the numbers in South Asian crowds
have grown exponentially, while the decorum of the Raj era
has turned into frenzied ecstasy. Political rallies are openly referred to as *tamashas* — shows — and politicians round up enormous crowds, sometimes by main force, to give the appearance
of mass support when the reality is lacking. (Indira Gandhi was
especially famous for this.) Benazir loved it all: she played the
crowd masterfully and drew inspiration and sustenance from its
palpable love.

Two days after her arrival she and her entourage set out on
a tour of the Punjab, visiting nineteen cities, including Jhelum,
known as the "city of soldiers" for the many men it had provided to the army, and Rawalpindi, home of the army general
headquarters and place of her father's execution. Everywhere
they were accorded the same ecstatic reception — to the disgust of the regime, which mandated that films and photographs
of the rallies not be disseminated in the official press and that
Bhutto's image not appear on Pakistani television. The group
then proceeded to Peshawar, near the Khyber Pass in the North-
West Frontier Province, the center for Afghan mujahideen activity in Pakistan and the place where many of Pakistan's three

million Afghan refugees were living. Then on to Balochistan. The sheer numbers of PPP supporters all over the country were so great that Bhutto's enemies in the regime did not dare interfere with her activities. But other PPP activists were harassed, arrested, even shot down.

Back in Karachi, Bhutto and the PPP reestablished their alliance with the Movement for the Restoration of Democracy; solidarity was vital if they were to have any chance against Zia. The group — more or less united, though the leaders of several other parties resented Bhutto's easy assumption that she would be the MRD's figurehead — agreed to stage rallies in the big cities on Independence Day, August 14, and pressed again for September elections. In the lead-up to August 14, anticipation built, with the foreign press flooding into Karachi. Bhutto's old Eliot House neighbor, the writer Anne Fadiman, arrived on August 8 to do a piece for *Life* magazine about her friend's return to Pakistan, accompanied by photographer Mary Ellen Mark. The two Americans looked on in astonishment as preparations for the coming battle swirled around them. "Her phones were tapped," Fadiman remembered. "A truck belonging to Pakistan's Central Intelligence Agency was routinely parked outside her gate."[3] Opposition workers and protesters were being arrested and beaten by the thousand. Benazir, undaunted and even excited, prepared for the day of protest.

She was planning to lead a car procession from Faisalabad to Lahore, but she was greeted at the Karachi airport with a restraining order forbidding her to travel to those cities. Undaunted, she returned to 70 Clifton, and on the big day, August 14, she and her entourage, which now included Fadiman and Mark, set out for the rally in two vans with sunroofs, careening through the Karachi streets where supporters in their thousands shouted, waved flags, and pressed against the car, shaking it. Young men pressed bleeding wounds against the car windows, showing her that they had been beaten by the police. Mary Ellen Mark recalled Benazir as "a daredevil; she loved the excitement of crowds and danger. She climbed up to stand through the sunroof, and she stood there like the Statue of Liberty, just like a big heroic statue. She was very brave, determined. She lived for that kind of excitement. She really had a sense of what a superstar is."[4]

As the vehicles made their slow way through the crowd the police fired on them with tear gas shells. Miraculously, the vans managed to evade their uninvited escort long enough to tour the poorer neighborhoods, though at one point Bhutto had surreptitiously to change cars. When the group reached 70 Clifton that evening, the police were there with a warrant to arrest Bhutto, who was charged with unlawful assembly and sentenced to thirty days in prison. Waving at the crowds, she got into the police car and headed off to solitary confinement in Landhi Jail, still smiling radiantly. Mark's photographs, which were published in *Life* soon afterward, show a glowing, joyful-looking woman: she has clearly loved every minute of the chase.

Zia disclaimed any knowledge of Bhutto's arrest, saying that the president, Muhammad Khan Junejo, had been in charge of the police action, but he affirmed his approval, even stating his opinion that Bhutto had received financial backing from foreign governments, specifically the USSR, for his overthrow. Bhutto's allies in the US Senate, handpicked by Peter Galbraith and Claiborne Pell, expressed outrage at her incarceration, but President Reagan offered congratulations to Zia on the steps he was taking toward "democracy." Bhutto's trial revealed that she had committed no illegal act, and the groundswell of support for her inside and outside the country made the administration consider it unwise to keep her incarcerated. Released on September 9, she toured the country again — and the threats against her life and attacks on her supporters continued. One MRD leader was axed to death, and in January there was an assassination attempt against Bhutto herself when her car was shot at on the road to Larkana. Bhutto was not in the car; unbeknownst to her would-be assassins, she had opted that day to travel by air.

If she aspired to become the leader of an Islamic nation, Benazir Bhutto was in a difficult position. As her father's daughter she had that invaluable link with a male leader, a patriarchal figure, and, at least according to her own account of the matter, he had singled her out as the most worthy child to follow in his footsteps. But this was not enough. A single woman in Pakistan simply lacked the social authority to command a nation; husbandless, Bhutto faced only the shakiest political future.

There was also the question of her image as a practicing Muslim, far more important for a woman who hoped to achieve high office in Pakistan than for a man. Her friend Catherine Drucker remembers her saying that "in our religion, there is an obligation to marry and have children." "This seemed very ambiguous," comments Drucker; "did she mean that she herself believed it, or that it was a political necessity?"[5]

Bhutto was now in her thirties, and while she had never shown any aversion to handsome men — her friends at Oxford and Harvard agree on this fact — she had sublimated matrimonial notions to her political struggle. There had been no place for a man in her life until this moment; in fact in *Shame,* his roman à clef about Pakistan, Salman Rushdie had dubbed the character based on Benazir the "Virgin Ironpants." Now, with real power in sight, a fiancé became the indispensable object. But how to get hold of the right one? Her reflections on the conundrum, here given in an interview with the *New York Times Magazine* in 1994, are unusually honest:

> I *couldn't* have a love match. I was under so much scrutiny. If my name had been linked with a man, it would have destroyed my political career. Actually, I had reconciled myself to a life without marriage or children for the sake of my ca-

reer. And then my brothers got married. I realized I didn't even have a home, that in the future I couldn't do politics when I had to ask permission from their wives as to whether I could use the dining room or the telephone. I couldn't rent a home because a woman living on her own can be suspected of all kinds of scandalous associations. So keeping in mind that many people in Pakistan looked to me, I decided to make a personal sacrifice in what I thought would be, more or less, a loveless marriage, a marriage of convenience. The surprising thing is that we are very close and that it's been a very good match.[6]

The traditional arranged marriage was an event that was normal for most Pakistanis but didn't quite fit the progressive, liberated image of the Bhutto family. Zulfikar and Nusrat, after all, had married for love, and against the wishes of the Bhutto clan. But perhaps in Pakistan it was more difficult for a woman, like Benazir, to flaunt her independence by choosing her own partner than it would have been for a man, like her father; men, after all, were acknowledged as the masters of their own fates. Keeping this in mind, an arranged marriage might have been not only the simplest solution to her problem but the most politically savvy as well. In any case, she seems to have felt the need to defend her decision to have an arranged marriage, particularly to Western observers, for she knew how important it was that she be perceived in Europe and America as the progressive, liberal face of the Muslim world. "People today do computer dating," she argued. "Is that a betrayal? When it's difficult to find a man, for whatever reason, one has to look for mediation . . . I'd love to arrange my own children's marriages. I say that because I've been so happy."[7]

All this is easy enough to explain. What is not so easy to comprehend, in retrospect, is the choice of Asif Ali Zardari for the male lead in this latest act of the family drama. Socially and professionally he was not a match for her. The Zardaris were a landowning family, but on a smaller scale than the Bhuttos. Asif's father had made a substantial fortune in construction; he also owned movie theaters in Karachi. Asif himself was good-looking, a passionate polo player, and reputed to be an almost equally enthusiastic womanizer. His education couldn't com-pare with Benazir's: he had attended a military cadet college near Hyderabad that catered to the sons of the rich, and had put in a few months at a commercial college in London, though upon the couple's engagement it was put about in the press that he had attended the London School of Economics. "I have no interest in politics," he informed the press, and this appears to have been a sincere statement at that time.[8]

Zardari had positive qualities that seemed to balance his lack of substance. Everyone remarked on his warmth: he was a kind man, genuinely friendly and concerned, socially adept, easygoing, lighthearted. In many ways he appeared the ideal political spouse, for at gatherings he could play the room, fill-ing glasses and cracking jokes, making every guest feel cared for, while his wife got on with business. He was also a singularly de-voted father — an important quality for the husband of a power-ful woman always on the move. And he had courage. To marry into the Bhutto family, the archenemies of the military dictator, was a very brave act, and Zardari was to pay dearly for it as well as to reap enormous benefits.

As Benazir's friend Christina Lamb, a British journalist who covered Pakistan at the time, noted, "Weddings in Pakistan are a matter of face. Combine that with Benazir's fanatical perfec-tionism, and you have a recipe for high tension."[9] Conscious that her every action at this time held a potential political sig-nificance, Benazir walked a fine line between tradition and pro-gressivism. In a traditional arranged marriage, the bride was not offered the opportunity to meet the groom before the marriage, but Benazir and Asif had met and approved each other before the match was agreed on: "I did meet him," Benazir informed the *New York Times*, "and because I felt he's nice and had a sense of humor and he seemed to be a tolerant person in that he could handle having a wife who had an independent career of her own, I thought it was wise to accept the proposal."[10] Nevertheless, she conformed to the tradition that throughout the year of family negotiations over the match and the months of preparation leading up to the wedding, she and Asif could not spend a single moment alone together.

Another change in tradition was Benazir's request that Nusrat forgo giving the customary dowry. The Zardaris would be receiving no rich prizes from the Bhuttos except for Benazir herself—a lucrative prize enough, to be sure, for Benazir would immediately bestow on her new husband the PPP ticket for the Lyari seat, center of the Bhuttos' Karachi power base and the first step in Zardari's own inexorable rise to power and self-enrichment. She also radically cut down on the usual trousseau. "Instead of the 21 to 51 sets of clothes usually presented to the bride," Lamb reports, "she had set the limit at only two. Instead of gold bangles all the way up each arm, she said she would wear glass, explaining: 'I am a leader—I must set an example to my people.' Nor, she said, did she have time for the traditional week's purdah. Instead she kept nipping out to the office."[11] More importantly, she decided to keep her maiden name: "Benazir Bhutto doesn't cease to exist the moment she gets married," she insisted. "I am not giving myself away. I belong to myself and I always shall."[12] This bold feminist gesture worked, of course, very much to her own advantage, for it would have been political folly to give up the magic name of Bhutto.

Wedding invitations were mailed from Dubai rather than Pakistan, lest the Zia regime confiscate them. Anne Fadiman, who arrived from America to attend her friend's wedding and cover it for *Life,* found herself "surprised and touched that as she prepared for her wedding, Benazir permitted herself to be unequivocally feminine for the first time in years ... She took considerable pleasure in having her hair and nails done, she experimented each day with different shades of eye makeup, and she giggled a lot, just the way she used to do when she was seventeen."[13] Every evening the Bhutto women and their female friends donned brightly colored *shalwar kameez* and danced, in preparation for the *Mehndi,* the evening of music and dance that would take place on the eve of the wedding. Benazir's Western guests agreed that they felt "like drab little caterpillars surrounded by butterflies ... [The atmosphere at 70 Clifton was a] gaudy, feverish, sentimental scene."[14]

During the *Mehndi,* Benazir and Zardari sat on a double throne under a steady rain of rose petals. At the actual exchange of vows, the *Nikah,* they sat on a dais covered by a veil. "A silver mirror was placed between them so that when the veil was removed, Asif would be the first to see his bride's downcast, reflected face."[15] The ceremony took place in the garden at 70 Clifton, before a surprisingly small group of family and friends: about a hundred, by one estimation. "Benazir was excited," remembers Yolanda Kodrzycki. "There was a chaotic situation afterward, a big mob scene with photographers pushing to get in."[16] After that, the celebration went public, with a nighttime party at an enormous sports field in the poor Karachi slum neighborhood of Lyari, where crowds approached two hundred thousand and the revelry grew riotous, with youthful PPP supporters storming the stage and shooting off Kalashnikovs into the air. The gunfire killed one bystander and injured more than thirty.

Just how happy a marriage Bhutto and Zardari enjoyed will probably never be known: rigorously protective of her image, Bhutto always projected support and loyalty for her unpopular mate. Of their twenty years as a couple, Zardari spent a total of ten in prison. The two were only infrequently together. For the last few years of Bhutto's life, even after Zardari's final release from prison in 2004, the couple lived apart, and a number of their "friends" confided to the press that the marriage was effectively over. But whatever the state of their personal relationship, there can be no doubt that the two of them worked together as a team throughout their two decades in and out of power. Bhutto, of course, had little choice in the matter. Divorce, or any open breach, would probably have spelled the end of her political career. "A Pakistani woman will endure almost anything in order to hold a marriage together," Bhutto's associate Tehmina Durrani has said. "In our society, marriage may be purgatory, but divorce is hell."[17]

ON MAY 29, 1988, Zia unexpectedly dissolved Parliament; fired his prime minister, Muhammad Khan Junejo; and called for elections within ninety days. Bhutto and the PPP doubted that the elections would be conducted honestly, but they prepared for them with optimism. It occurred to Bhutto that the election date might have been chosen cynically; she had recently announced that she was expecting a baby, and the dates Zia had set for the elections seemed likely to coincide with her delivery. The PPP went to the Supreme Court to challenge Zia's 1985 voter registration clause, which permitted the administration to disallow a party from participating in elections on flimsy grounds, and Bhutto went on an energetic PR tour of the country, despite her pregnancy and the summer heat. The success of the PPP made Zia begin to panic, and in July he announced that candidates could only run as individuals, not party members. The PPP and the other parties that made up the MRD struggled to keep up with the barrage of conflicting presidential decrees.

But suddenly, on August 17, 1988, all the rules of the Pakistani political game were rewritten. Zia had been at a military base near Bahawalpur that morning to watch a demonstration of the new Abrams tank from the United States. (The demonstration turned out to be a disaster, with the tank missing its target every time it fired.) That afternoon he boarded Pak One, a Lockheed C-130 aircraft, getting into the VIP capsule with several other Very Important People: General Akhtar Abdul Rehman, the chairman of the Joint Chiefs of Staff and, as head of the ISI, the architect of the Afghan war against the Soviets and organizer of the mujahideen network; General Mohamed Afzal, chief of the general staff; the American ambassador, Arnold L. Raphel; General Herbert M. Wassom, the head of the US military aid mission to Pakistan; and eight other Pakistani generals. The vice-chief-of-staff, Lieutenant General Aslam Beg, was the only top member of the chain of command not on board; he was flying back to Islamabad in his own jet.

The plane took off; almost immediately, ground control at Bahawalpur was unable to reach the pilots. Eighteen miles away, the plane was seen to be out of control, swerving and diving. It finally plunged nose first into the ground and exploded. All thirty people on board died in the flames. Aslam Beg, flying nearby in his own jet, witnessed the accident and returned post haste to Islamabad, where he quickly took control of government buildings and television stations.

Investigation indicated sabotage, very possibly with a gas bomb planted in the air vent to incapacitate the pilots. Traces of pentaerythritol tetranitrate, a high explosive, were found. The murder of Zia and his fellow passengers has never been solved: as Edward Jay Epstein, the journalist who did a major investigative piece on the incident for *Vanity Fair,* has pointed out, "It was not unlike Agatha Christie's thriller *Murder on the Orient Express,* in which, if one looked hard enough, everyone aboard the train had a motive for the murder."[1] First there were the Soviets, who had every reason to want to dispose of America's favorite Cold War ally. Then there was India, which resented Zia's supplying of Sikh separatists with weapons. (Prime Minister Rajiv Gandhi's mother, Prime Minister Indira Gandhi, had been assassinated by Sikh terrorists four years previously.)

John Gunther Dean, the American ambassador to India at the time, publicly suspected the Israeli secret agency Mossad of being the assassins — they were hoping to put a stop to the Pakistani nuclear program — as did Barbara Crossette, *New York Times* South Asia bureau chief from 1988 to 1991, who wrote a probing piece in *World Policy Journal* on the subject.[2] Then of course there was the usual suspect, al-Zulfikar; it had initially taken credit for sabotaging the plane, though Murtaza retracted this statement after he discovered the American ambassador had been on board. Epstein himself inclined to the theory that it was an inside job organized by the Pakistani military, for neither Zia nor Rehman had wanted to go to Bahawalpur but had been pressured to do so by the army command. The Pakistani military authorities in their turn tried to put the blame on Shi'ite extremists. And what of the Americans? Had they grown tired of their favorite bulwark against communism? The Muslim bomb, after all, was still being actively developed despite Washington's sticks and carrots.

Police investigation was derailed in the usual Pakistani style. No autopsies were performed on the victims. And despite the deaths of Ambassador Raphel and General Wassom, US secretary of state George Schultz requested that the FBI keep out of the investigation. Whether or not the United States was directly or indirectly involved, the perception in Washington seemed to be that a thorough investigation of the disaster might turn up all kinds of unsavory information that the world had better not know. Its policy now was to close the door on the sketchy, compromised past and to back a post-Zia Pakistan with an attractive, secular, American-educated young woman as its leading political figure. The 250 pages of documents related to Zia's death in the US National Archives are still classified.

Bhutto herself, according to Christopher Hitchens's account of his conversation with her after her first election victory, chose to believe that it was none other than the Deity himself who had rid the world of this evil man.

> "You'll think this sounds irrational and unscientific, but I think the death of Zia was an act of God. An. Act. Of. God. First they said there was a missile that hit the plane. No evidence of a missile found. Then it was a bomb. No evidence of a bomb. Now they say there must have been gas to knock out the crew. But I think you should read the section of the Koran about Pharaoh the tyrant, where it says, 'Look for him in the sky, you won't find him; look for him on the earth, you won't find him.' Zia has disappeared in *flames*. He denied our family the Muslim right to a last look at my father's dead face. Well, no one saw *his* dead face. And the plane"—here she leans forward very intently—"the plane that crashed was the one that flew my father's body from the jail where he was hanged in Rawalpindi. And the only thing not burned in the wreck was the Holy Koran." She sits back. "God gives the tyrant a rope, but he *tugs* it in the end."[3]

Plenty of people all over the world breathed a sigh of relief at Zia's death, but Benazir Bhutto was its most obvious beneficiary. She was no longer politically shackled to her father's murderer; she need not run for office as prime minister to his president. And now her luck continued to hold. Zia had ordered elections for November, perhaps assuming that by then she would be ready to deliver her baby and unable to campaign vigorously. In the event, her son, Bilawal Zardari, was born on September 21, allowing his mother plenty of time to build up steam for the November election.

The feeling of hope that surged through liberal Pakistani society may have been irrational, but the return of democracy, in however compromised a form, was truly a magical moment.

The novelist Kamila Shamsie, a teenager at that time, later recalled the spirit of 1988 rather ruefully:

> Given the state of Pakistan today [2010], it is impossible to remember the heady days at the end of 1988 without tasting ashes. Elation was in the air, and it had a soundtrack. At parties my friends and I continued to dance to the UK's Top 40, but the songs that ensured everyone crowded on to the dance floor were "Dil Dil Pakistan" and the election songs of both Benazir's Pakistan People's Party and the Karachi-based Muhajir Qaumi Movement (MQM). There was little concern for political affiliation. At one such party I recall a young Englishman looking perplexed as Karachi's teens gyrated to a song with the chorus *Jeay jeay jeay Bhutto Benazir* ("Long live Benazir"). "I can't imagine a group of schoolkids in London dancing to a 'Long live Maggie' number," he said, and I pitied him and all the English teenagers for not knowing what it was like to see the dawn of democracy.[4]

The heady atmosphere of the election, with surging crowds of adoring supporters greeting Bhutto at the series of rallies she held all over the country, was a period unlike any other in Pakistani history. She carried out a grueling campaign schedule with the tireless zeal of her father, despite the interruption of Bilawal's birth. As the unchallenged figurehead of the PPP (Nusrat, perhaps reluctantly, had ceded her dominant role to her more energetic daughter), she was now in a position to re-create it in her own image, and it was an image that should have given the traditionally leftist power base of the PPP pause. Her choice of landowners and other power brokers for places on the party ticket reflected not only the apparently unshakeable inequities of Pakistani society but her own values as well.

And while the world, and idealistic Pakistanis like the young

Kamila Shamsie and her friends, might have seen a progressive woman about to accede to the kind of power that would enable her to change her troubled country for good, the reality was rather different, as Bhutto must have known from the beginning. As the example of her father had proved more than a decade previously, no civilian can lead Pakistan without striking some sort of deal with the military, and Zia's sudden exit from the scene had left the country under the rule of three men who were implacably hostile to parliamentary democracy. First, there was General Aslam Beg, who had so providentially escaped the fatal plane crash and had now taken over as the new army chief. Then there was the head of the ISI, Lieutenant General Hamid Gul, described memorably by the American journalist Lawrence Wright as "a short man with a rigid, military posture and raptor-like features"[5]; he had helped oversee the creation of the Taliban (his special protégé was the Pashtun warlord Gulbuddin Hekmatyar) and openly supported it right up until 9/11. And finally there was the new president, Ghulam Ishaq Khan, the chairman of the Senate who had ascended to the presidency after Zia's death, according to constitutional regulation. A civilian figure, Ishaq Khan had nevertheless worked closely with the military throughout his career and had been a key aide to Zia.

These three men, often referred to by journalists as a "troika," were fearful that a liberal civilian government, given any real power, would reduce the military budget and perhaps even shelve the all-important nuclear program. With these fears predominating, Aslam Beg contacted Bhutto, pledging his commitment to fair and timely elections *if* she would agree to reinstate him as army chief in the event of her election. Other conditions were also exacted. The defense budget would be nonnegotiable; Ishaq Khan would stay in office as president to her prime minister; Zia's foreign minister, Yakub Ali Khan, would also stay in office. The army would hold the ultimate veto in security and foreign matters. The civilian government would have no say in the nation's Afghan policy, and the nuclear program would stay entirely under the control of the military. With little choice in the matter, Bhutto hurriedly agreed to the terms. The implications of that agreement were to be more serious than she might have realized.

In the meantime, the troika had not abandoned hopes that Bhutto might yet be defeated at the polls. As she pointed out in her autobiography, she and other PPP insiders were shocked "when Ishaq Khan kept the caretaker government consisting of Zia's cronies and henchmen. Instead of a neutral and impartial cabinet, these were the same representatives of Zia's corrupt system to whom fair and impartial elections would mean the end of their own power and patronage."[6] The Supreme Court had ruled against Zia's injunction preventing candidates with party affiliations from running for office, and the troika now supported a coalition of parties that opposed the dominant PPP. The most notable of these was the ISI-backed IJI, the Islami Jamhoori Ittehad (Islamic Democratic Alliance).

Bhutto confronted Islamist fears about women leaders head-on, in her best Oxford Union fighting style, asserting that women were, if anything, even better qualified than men to act as a nation's parent figure. "Sovereignty belongs to God," she stated later. "Men and women are his trustees. The trustees vote for a government. Therefore, as the trustees have voted for a government, that government has come into being by the will of Allah, and is an expression of his sovereignty. So it is Islamic to have a government led by a woman."[7] This was good casuistry but by no means reassuring to hard-core Islamists, who found Bhutto threatening not only on principle, as a woman, but also in particular, as her secularist father's daughter.

Peter Galbraith, who had flown to Pakistan as part of a delegation to monitor the elections, joined the Bhutto-Zardari clan in Larkana on election day. "That night we were in her living room at Larkana," Galbraith recalled.

> Benazir was in the corner on the phone, getting the results precinct by precinct . . . And initially the results came in and they began to show a rather large win for the PPP. As that became clear, it began to slow down. The next day it had emerged that she had [94 seats, so it was short of a majority, but the next party, the Muslim League, had about 55]. The attitude among her advisers was that they'd been robbed. This is the mentality of people who have spent their entire life in opposition. They're always seeing the regime as trying to screw them, as indeed it was. And I'm sure that there were robbed seats, I think that's quite clear. [The press officer] wrote up a press statement for Benazir to give complaining about the results. In Bahawalpur and Sargodha they'd been robbed, so they should have had more seats in Punjab. And Benazir gave this to me to look at, I looked at it, and I said, "Well, I'm sure this is true. But I can guarantee you that the international journalists who are outside the wall — CNN, ABC, CBS, BBC, German TV — none of those guys know where Sargodha and Bahawalpur are. And while they know where the Punjab is, their viewers don't. They've come here to cover this incredible story about this young woman who is now about to become the first elected prime minister of a Muslim country. Instead of complaining about how you've been robbed, why don't you tell them you won?"[8]

She quickly saw the point and asked Galbraith to draft an acceptance speech for her. "I wrote up the most conventional of statements — 'the People have spoken' — 'it's the heaviest of responsibilities . . .'" he said. "Then we left — abruptly — to the airport. Dusk had fallen, and the airport was I think twenty-five miles away. When we left, there were people all along the route . . . Ten deep, cheering. It was so moving . . . And then we landed in Karachi, and there were half a million people on the tarmac."[9]

In the final tally, the PPP had taken 94 out of the 207 seats in the National Assembly; the runner-up was the IJI, with 56. This was a very good result for the PPP, but not quite as good as it might have been, for the party achieved an outright majority only in its home province of Sindh. The IJI had control of the Punjab, Pakistan's largest and most powerful province, and its new chief minister was a man who would prove Bhutto's principal political rival for the rest of her career: Nawaz Sharif, the powerful, conservative Lahore businessman who had been a protégé of Zia's. "Sharif's election campaign," writes Husain Haqqani, "had unleashed a xenophobic Pakistani nationalism tinged with more Islamism than had previously been the norm in Pakistani politics. Ideas nurtured under Zia's authoritarian rule now had a democratic manifestation. Beg and Gul could keep Bhutto in check by pitting the Punjab provincial government against the prime minister."[10] Once the new National Assembly was in place, the Inter-Services Intelligence attempted to lure newly elected PPP legislators to defect to the IJI.

And the troika had not yet accepted the inevitable. On November 19, the PPP won the most seats in the Provincial Assemblies, as well as the National, 184 seats to the IJI's 145. Still no word from Ishaq Khan, who as president was now constitutionally obliged to call on the leader of the party with the largest number of votes to form a government. Unwilling to instate Bhutto, he was playing for time, while the military approached elected PPP members and tried to persuade them to defect from the party and bring as many of their fellow members as possible with them. The troika even considered asking Nusrat Bhutto to form a government — they felt that the rather tired older lady, still recovering from her cancer treatments, would prove

far more malleable than her aggressive, energized daughter—
and Nusrat, somewhat surprisingly, did not dismiss the idea: so
much for Benazir's assertion that her mother had never wanted
power.

Two weeks went by in this waiting game, during which time
Bhutto wrote a letter to the international community laying
out the situation. She had Mark Siegel, her lobbyist, pass out
copies of this letter to members of the US Congress, and PPP
party members in Britain and Europe provided copies to leading MPs.

Inevitably, it was not the will of the Pakistani people but
the will of Washington that finally budged Ishaq Khan. He had
no option but to yield when the US ambassador, Bob Oakley,
phoned him and insisted that he ask Bhutto to form a government. Ishaq Khan's inability to resist this demand only showed
the truth in the old Pakistani saying that the most important
person in the country is not the head of state, or even the army
chief, but the American ambassador—known to cynical Islamabad insiders as "the Viceroy."

BENAZIR BHUTTO TOOK the oath of office on December 2, 1988, becoming, at thirty-five years of age, the youngest prime minister in Pakistani history as well as the first woman. "The people of Pakistan," she would write in her autobiography with only a bit of justifiable hubris, "had rejected bigotry and prejudice in electing a woman Prime Minister. It was an enormous honor, and an equally enormous responsibility . . . I had not asked for this role; I had not asked for this mantle. But the forces of destiny and the forces of history had thrust me forward, and I felt privileged and awed."[1] Elation washed over the country, with cries of "*Bhutto ki tasveer — Benazir, Benazir*" ("Benazir is Bhutto's true incarnation") heard throughout Pakistan. American and European media portrayed a triumphant and inspirational leader, a potent symbol of hope to a country in deep trouble.

In retrospect, though, it can be seen that while the American press paid lip service to this miracle of democracy, and were certainly impressed by Benazir's glamour and panache, their true concerns, as ever, were with American interests. On the *MacNeil/Lehrer NewsHour* Robert MacNeil "defined" Pakistan for his presumably ignorant American viewers simply as "the strategically placed Moslem nation that has played a key role in supplying the anti-Soviet side in the Afghan War,"[2] and he consistently derailed Bhutto's efforts to discuss the three million Afghan refugees who had flooded into Pakistan, grilling her instead on her proposed policies vis-à-vis the Soviet Union. When she tried to sidestep the question gracefully, saying "We do not feel that good relations with one country need necessarily preclude good relations with another," MacNeil reverted to fears about an Islamic bomb — to which Benazir responded earnestly, and with no truth whatsoever, that Pakistan had no intention of procuring a bomb and that her government "would like to see the whole region emerge as a weapons-free, nuclear-weapons-free zone."[3]

Bhutto understood the value of the big political gesture in garnering national and international good will. Upon taking office she released all political prisoners — of whom Zia had assembled a great many — and immediately relaxed government censorship. She also reinstated the rights of labor unions and student unions, which had gone underground during the Zia years. And in a truly bold move, she invited Prime Minister Rajiv Gandhi of India and his wife, Sonia, to be her guests at Islamabad, where they stayed on after the summit meeting of the South Asian Association for Regional Cooperation. Bhutto was well aware of the Pakistani military's paranoid distrust of Indian leaders, but tensions over Kashmir were once again at a boiling point and she felt the invitation to be judicious; too high a level of tension might give the military the excuse they were always seeking to step in once again. As the junior members of prominent political dynasties, both of whose parents had met violent deaths, Gandhi and Bhutto had much in common and their meeting was cordial. (Predictably, though, when they met behind closed doors Bhutto's political enemies tried to stir up Islamist outrage by suggesting that the two were enjoying a sexual relationship. They also reminded fearful Islamists that Bhutto had had a Hindu grandmother, which, they implied, made her something less than a wholehearted Muslim.)

However good Bhutto's intentions were, though, it was

soon clear that, as with the accession of her father to power seventeen years previously, the sense of strength projected by the image of a charismatic leader masked a very different reality. In Pakistan no civilian president has been able to control the army, and since the beginning of the war in Afghanistan, the ISI and other covert services had vastly extended their powers. Throughout the Zia years these services, along with the military high command, had handled the tricky problems of Afghanistan, India, and Kashmir, and they meant to keep it that way. Bhutto the Younger, for all her bravado, was going into office with only very limited room for action, and the troika intended to block even that. On her first days in office, Shyam Bhatia has reported, "not a single file was brought to her for comment or a decision. When Benazir brought this to [Ishaq] Khan's attention, his response was one of indifference. It was only when Benazir threatened to go public with her concerns that Khan ordered government civil servants to include the prime minister in the decision-making process by sending her relevant documents for discussion and approval."[4]

There was also the problem of implementing the many reforms Bhutto had promised voters. All election pledges are necessarily suspect, but her forty-two-section party manifesto was more than usually pie-in-the-sky, considering the budget she was going to have to work with. She had assured the electorate that under PPP rule, Pakistan — still with less than half its adult population able to read and write — would have a universal education system as well as universal health care, and that half a million new homes would be constructed per year. The Pakistani government, she implied, would also ensure that each citizen received adequate food, clothing, and housing under her administration. According to one calculation, her manifesto would require a welfare program thirty-three times the size of the aid package at that time being provided by the United States to Pakistan — and only 1 percent of the Pakistani population, mostly from the middle class, actually paid taxes! In any case, with the collapse of the Soviet Union soon after Bhutto's accession and the withdrawal of its army from Afghanistan, American largesse to its ally quickly dried up. By 1989 Pakistan was suffering from inflation, high unemployment, and a serious drug problem, for in the wake of the Afghan war Pakistan had become a major manufacturer of heroin: between 1979 and the mid-1980s the number of Pakistani heroin addicts soared from about ten thousand to half a million, and in 1999 they were said to number between three and four million.[5] As Abida Hussein, a member of the opposition alliance, remarked, "I tend to feel that if Benazir Bhutto had a perfect head, perfect heart and a perfect soul she'd probably still fail."[6]

It was quickly becoming evident that she possessed none of those qualities. Since her student days, observers, even those who were most fond of her, had noticed that style tended to trump substance. "She was bright but not at all a policy wonk type," remembers Catherine Drucker:

> To her, I think that policy was something that underlings wrote up, with boxes to tick for action at the bottom of the page. I remember being a little shocked when she said something to this effect to me once. She saw the role of leader, I think, as being charismatic, as pulling together alliances in a personal way... She could also be gullible. At one time, during her years at the Barbican, she went, under an assumed name, to some ridiculous course about influencing people. It was not quite the Moonies, but some absurd charlatan, all the same. Well, I was such a prig and intellectual snob, I thought it was on a level with watching *Dallas* — which she also did.[7]

Bhutto's nominally socialist agenda was designed to recall that of her father's PPP. But by 1988 the world had changed. Benazir Bhutto's government, notes Tariq Ali, "came into power in Pakistan in a new world — a neoliberal world. This is a world where only money matters, a world when politicians all over the world are seen as corrupt and linked intimately to corporations."[8] Bhutto was not a natural socialist, or even as adept at talking the talk as Zulfikar had been. In fact she disagreed with many of her father's socialist economic policies and tried to privatize a number of industries that had been nationalized during the 1970s, although she had little success on this front during her first term. She also reversed the admittedly limited progress her father had made in land reform by removing the ceilings he had set on land holdings. During her years in power she would never seriously challenge the feudal system, which had managed to hold firm through imperial, nationalist civilian, military, and "socialist" governments.

One ominous signal was sent out very early in Bhutto's tenure, when she appointed her mother as senior minister without portfolio, her father-in-law as chairman of the Parliamentary Public Accounts Committee, and, rather astonishingly, *herself* as the new treasury minister. If there had been hopes that the country's entrenched crony capitalism and backroom political fixing might be swept away with a new broom, these subsided quickly. Bhutto also created a so-called Placement Bureau that allowed her, as prime minister, to make senior appointments to the civil service.

Z. A. Bhutto's associates, the old guard of the PPP, might have supported Benazir's candidacy, but they were not all on board with the new agenda, and several of them left the party, including the family patriarch Mumtaz Ali Bhutto and a key architect of the 1973 constitution, Hafeez Pirzada. Benazir's highhandedness as well as her policy shifts might have disturbed them; after she became prime minister she expected PPP workers to address her as *Mohtarma* — "respected lady." Disillusioned members of the old PPP dropped out of the party; others, not viewed as sufficiently useful to the agenda of the new PPP, were not given party tickets to stand in the general election. Many of these were replaced by men whom Fatima Bhutto, admittedly a partisan historian, has described as a "core of personal business contacts and establishment politicians who trimmed their sails to the prevailing political wind and who would soon become the new party's power brokers."[9]

Unable to get much done at home, Bhutto set out on a series of foreign visits in an effort to strengthen alliances, present the new face of Pakistan to the world press, and attract foreign aid and investment. She went out of her way to maintain good relations with her father's allies in the Arab world, leaders such as Muammar Qaddafi of Libya, Sheikh Zayed of Abu Dhabi, and the Saudi royal family. Particularly important on her itinerary was a visit to the United States in June 1989, a masterpiece of public relations and good will during which she addressed both houses of Congress and gave the commencement speech at Harvard. Anne Fadiman, who accompanied Bhutto's entourage, remembers some incongruous scenes. At a dinner given for Bhutto by Vice President Dan Quayle, for instance, American guests were rather embarrassed when the host "read his speech like a first-grader" while the visiting Pakistani leader delivered a sophisticated and "rhetorically subtle" address. At another grand party Fadiman chatted with singer Andy Williams, who had no idea why he had been invited; it turned out that Bhutto's fixers had got him confused with her beloved Neil Diamond.[10]

Most Americans who met her found Bhutto attractive and inspirational, but at high government levels there was not much confidence in this untried young woman; the State Department and CIA, in particular, much preferred to deal with the devils they knew: Beg, Gul, and Ishaq Khan. The hundreds of millions of dollars of aid they were still funneling through Pakistan to the Afghan guerrillas continued to be controlled by Gul, as director of the ISI.

Bhutto's first year in office saw an extended power struggle between herself and the troika, in which she won some battles but ultimately lost the war. Both the army and the intelligence services saw Bhutto-style populism as their natural enemy, a threat to the autonomous powers they had enjoyed under Ayub, Yahya, and Zia. Under the Pakistani constitution the president, rather than the prime minister, had the authority to appoint senior army officers and civil servants and even to dismiss the prime minister if he thought fit. Three months after the general election, with the presidential election looming, Bhutto had candidates she preferred to Ishaq Khan, but she unwisely let herself be pressured into backing Ishaq instead. Once back in office, Ishaq insisted that he and only he had the prerogative to make senior military appointments.

But Bhutto was nothing if not combative, and in May 1989 she unexpectedly asserted her authority by sacking Hamid Gul and replacing him with a retired general whom she trusted to keep her more in the intelligence loop. Gul's toppling from power had been precipitated by a failed operation on the Afghan border and a widespread suspicion that the ISI and MI (Military Intelligence) had been plotting a coup against Bhutto. Even after his departure, however, the anti-Bhutto intrigues continued, and later in the year the ISI launched a secret offensive they code-named Operation Midnight Jackal: an attempt to prevent National Assembly members from voting with the PPP through bribery and intimidation.

More trouble arose when armed resistance to Indian rule broke out throughout the Kashmir Valley in the summer of 1989. Kashmiris claimed that elections two years earlier had been rigged, and militant groups began to form throughout the region, calling either for the independence of Jammu and Kashmir or for its incorporation into Pakistan. Bhutto and her government supported the disgruntled Kashmiris, and Bhutto called once more for the UN plebiscite that had been promised in 1948 but had never taken place.

Tensions between India and Pakistan always threatened to go nuclear, assuming Pakistan had the wherewithal to make the bomb; its only chance of winning a war against the overwhelmingly superior Indian military machine would be a preemptive nuclear attack. Just how knowledgeable Bhutto was about her country's nuclear program has never been quite clear. During her Washington visit she had to be briefed about its progress by CIA director William Webster, who showed her a mock-up of the Pakistani bomb; work on it had reached a crescendo in recent years, with Zia and the military well aware that American aid might dry up if the Soviet Union collapsed. Now that the Soviets were no longer threatening Afghanistan, President George H. W. Bush decided the time had come to tell Bhutto that Pakistan could not continue to receive military aid unless she assured him that her government would forbear from producing nuclear bomb cores, the final step in the process. Bush did, however, say that he would authorize the sale to Pakistan of sixty F-16 planes. Bhutto told the US Congress, as she had told the American press the previous year and with about as much truth, "We do not possess nor do we intend to make a nuclear device. That is our policy"[11]—although Mark Siegel informed *The New Yorker*'s Seymour Hersh that Bhutto had been shaken up, during her briefing with Webster, to find how little she actually knew about the program.

Now it seemed that Pakistan and India, where Rajiv Gandhi's government had recently been replaced by that of V. P. Singh, might really be heading for a nuclear collision. In January 1990, Indian police opened fire on pro-independence demonstrators in Kashmir, killing fifty of them and causing an uproar in Kashmir. The Pakistani military were operating training camps on their side of the border for "freedom fighters," and Bhutto, in a nakedly jingoistic move, visited one of these training camps and pledged nearly $5 million to help the militants in their cause, then followed up this move with a series of speeches in their defense all around the country. At around this time, CIA operatives noticed indications that India was moving its troops to within fifty miles of the Pakistani border and that General Beg had authorized the technicians at the Pakistani nuclear base, Kahuta, to complete the final step in the construction of a nuclear weapon. Seymour Hersh, who researched and wrote about the incident for *The New Yorker* in 1993, quoted one intelligence analyst as saying that the Pakistanis "had F-16s pre-positioned and armed for delivery — on full alert, with pilots in the aircraft. I believed that they were ready to launch on command and that the message had been clearly conveyed to the Indians. We're saying, 'Oh, shit.' "[12]

Bush sent Robert Gates to South Asia as his special envoy to meet with both Indian and Pakistani leaders and try to defuse the situation. In the end this approach worked, though Bhutto, amazingly, couldn't be bothered to see him: she was touring the Gulf states to gain their support for Kashmiri elections and was in Yemen at the time of Gates's visit, offhandedly suggesting that he join her there. Instead, Gates met with Ishaq Khan, informing him that should Pakistan go to war with India, no American help would be forthcoming. The crisis was averted, and Pakistan, knuckling under American pressure, agreed to shut down the training camps for Kashmiri militants.

Bhutto's handling of the situation was poor: she purposely fanned anti-Indian aggression, then left the real negotiations to be dealt with by others. She might have played her role with more dignity, but her behavior is indicative of her real position; it was the military hierarchy that was calling the shots, not she.

DISILLUSION WITH THE new Bhutto regime had set in only months after her 1988 election. Kamila Shamsie, speaking for a generation of liberal young people who came of age during Bhutto's first term, remembers the signs.

A few months into the tenure of the Bhutto government, with the new head of state's approval, Pakistan TV organized and recorded a concert called *Music '89* . . . Tens of millions of people tuned in and religio-fascists fulminated from every pulpit. Benazir, as she would go on to do time and again, gave in to the demands of the religious right and, despite its huge success, the tapes of *Music '89* were removed from the PTV library.

One of the most distinguishing features of the Bhutto government was the prevalence of the status quo precisely where there was the most urgent need for change. Islamization was no longer the government's spoken objective, but all the madrasas, jihadi groups and reactionary preachers continued as if nothing had changed, with the support of the army and intelligence services . . . The great social transformation we had expected to see, that Return to Before, never happened.

Even worse, many of the changes begun by Zia ul-Haq
gained momentum . . .[1]

It turned out that whatever Bhutto's intentions might have
been, with so narrow a majority she was never able to muster
enough support in the National Assembly to roll back the Islamist tide Zia had released. Hence what was perhaps the worst
blot on her record: failure to suspend the dreadful Hudood Ordinances, which would continue as the law of the land until
2006. She also purported to be pro-life. Such positions lost her
the support of many Pakistani feminists, and in fact at no time
in her years in power did Bhutto, Westernized though she was,
feel comfortable in seriously challenging Pakistan's Islamists.
Fatima Bhutto has expressed cynicism about her aunt's decision
to cover her head with a white *dupatta:* "She was the first member of our family to wear a *hijab,*" she comments acidly. "Benazir's choice was the first of its kind; not even her mother Nusrat
covered her hair; it was a choice designed to keep the Islamic
parties and leaders . . . on her side. Islam was an accessory at
times and at others, it seems, an ideology."[2]

Bhutto's administration by this time was embroiled in the ethnic clashes that were rocking her native province of Sindh, particularly Karachi, where the Urdu-speaking *muhajirs* were particularly numerous and powerful, making up a large portion of the
population. In 1984 a *muhajir* political party had been founded,
the Muhajir Qaumi Mahaz (Muhajir People's Movement).

The MQM had done well in Sindh in the 1988 elections,
and Bhutto's government had struck an agreement with them
in which they agreed to protect the party's political rights and
implement their development goals, among other things. Late
in 1989 the MQM, feeling that the government had not kept its
part of the deal, broke its alliance with the PPP, joined the opposition, and called for a general strike the next year.

Bhutto's failure to divest herself of President Ghulam Ishaq Khan proved to have been a great mistake when on August 7, 1990, he availed himself of his powers under the Eighth Amendment of the Pakistani constitution to dismiss her government on charges of corruption, nepotism, and despotism. A caretaker government under Ghulam Mustafa Jatoi, a former PPP member who had left the party, was sworn in, and Ishaq Khan promptly declared a state of emergency, citing "a threat to the security of Pakistan by external aggression and internal disturbances."[3] He called for new elections to be held as soon as possible. Bhutto was, for the moment, in the wilderness. She and her husband were prohibited from leaving the country.

The ISI had been actively spying on Bhutto throughout her twenty months in power, bugging her meetings and even videotaping her in private moments with her husband, as journalist Seymour Hersh has revealed. Corruption inquiries had focused not so much on Bhutto herself as on her husband and his father, who both proved to have done suspiciously well in financial ventures and real estate investments since assuming their governmental positions.

While there can be no doubt that the investigation into Benazir Bhutto's and Asif Ali Zardari's finances was politically motivated — a report from the auditor general of Pakistan reveals that Ishaq Khan paid plaintiffs to file corruption cases against the couple — neither has there ever been any doubt of Asif Ali Zardari's corruption. It was at this time that he gained the nickname of "Mr. Ten Percent" for his habit of taking kickbacks and skimming off the top of the many business and defense deals in which he was involved. Money laundering was among the many charges leveled at him, although when he was actually arrested, shortly after his wife's government was dismissed, it was because he had been accused of attaching a remote-controlled bomb to the leg of a businessman and sending him into a bank to withdraw funds for a kickback — an allegation that was never substantiated. Zardari was taken into custody on October 10 on charges of extortion and spent the next three years there, although he won election to the National Assembly from his jail cell later that month. In those elections, the majority went to the Islami Jamhoori Ittehad, the conservative coalition that had been formed two years previously to defeat the renascent PPP, and Nawaz Sharif assumed the office of prime minister. Bhutto became leader of the opposition.

It was a role in which she proved effective, as she had been under Zia. Increasingly adept at playing the media and influencing public opinion, she attacked the conservative Sharif government on its every policy. While her own social programs had not been in any way effective, Sharif's were no better, and she spiritedly assaulted his dismal record on poverty, unemployment, and health care throughout his term in office. Sharif also failed to maintain order in Sindh province, where the MQM continued to stir up *muhajir* rage and unrest. Sharif and the IJI retaliated against Bhutto and Zardari with a vicious smear campaign, but the public was aware of the political motivations behind the attacks; as Sharif floundered in office, people were starting to forget the sins of the PPP and wish them back in office. Bhutto urged her followers to take their complaints into the streets, and in 1992 she organized what was supposed to have been a ten-day march against IJI rule, from Rawalpindi to Islamabad. Sharif had her placed under house arrest in an attempt to quash popular uprisings.

In spite of relentless pressure from Bhutto and the PPP, however, Sharif's fall from power was most likely precipitated by the same inherent problems with the Pakistani constitution that had brought down Bhutto herself. Ishaq Khan was still the country's president, and the balance of power between president and prime minister was as ill defined and contentious as ever. Inevitably the relations between the two men soured. Sharif was eventually compelled to resign, under pressure from the armed forces. In doing so, however, he managed to wangle an agreement by which Ishaq Khan, too, had to leave office. The army formed an interim government, with a general election three months later. The results, when tallied, recalled those of 1988: the PPP won more seats than any other one party but fell short, once again, of an outright majority, winning 86 seats against 73 for Sharif's PML (N) (The parenthetical N stands for Nawaz.) Bhutto was once again prime minister, but due to her narrow victory she had a weaker mandate than she had had in 1988 and would face strong resistance within the National Assembly.

She was sworn in on October 19, 1993. One mistake she was determined not to make again was to let herself be saddled with an adversarial president, and this time she exercised her prime ministerial power to select someone she believed to be malleable and apolitical: Farooq Leghari, landowner, one-time civil servant, longtime PPP member, and Z. A. Bhutto associate. Her hope was that Leghari would provide an adequate figurehead for the government while at the same time loyally serving Bhutto's own interests.

Hopes pinned on a Bhutto regime were much more limited in 1993 then they had been five years previously. As Najam Sethi, editor of Pakistan's *Friday Times* newsweekly, wrote of Bhutto and her opponent, Nawaz Sharif, "Both of them have done so badly in the past, it will be very difficult for them to do worse now." If a Bhutto government was to fail, he added, "everyone knows there will be no new elections. The army will take over."[4]

During Bhutto's first term she had tried honestly, if not always intelligently or with true purpose, to improve Pakistan's economy and political culture. In her second, there seemed almost nothing she could do. The public debt, which by 1996 included $32 billion in foreign loans, soaked up 70 percent of national revenues; the nonnegotiable military budget absorbed the rest. There was literally nothing left with which to implement the social programs Bhutto had pledged to deliver.

Another mistake Bhutto was determined not to make again was to be left out of the military loop. In later years she would make a startling admission to Shyam Bhatia: that she was, in her own words, "the mother of the missile programme."[5] Upon her return to office in 1993, there was consternation in army circles because the Indians had recently developed the long-range Agni missile, capable of hitting Pakistan's major cities. To counter these, the Pakistanis would need an equally powerful launch platform for their own nuclear warheads. North Korea had missile technology the Pakistanis needed, and the North Koreans, in turn, were in need of the enrichment secrets that A. Q. Khan had purloined from European laboratories.

Bhutto, due to travel to North Korea at the end of 1993, told Bhatia that she had been asked by the military, and had agreed, to carry nuclear data to Pyongyang on CDs for delivery to the North Koreans, and "implied, with a glint in her eye," that she had then brought North Korean missile information back with her to Pakistan, on more CDs. She said that in Islamabad she had bought an overcoat with the "deepest possible pockets" for the purpose. Six months after this initial interview with Bhatia, Bhutto agreed to give him an official one, on the record, but by then her story had changed, and she claimed that the Pakistanis had purchased the North Korean data for cash rather than barter and denied that she had played spy or carried the CDs. "Okay, thank you," she said to him. "I didn't carry it — symbolically, symbolically."[6]

In office for the second time, and with few illusions about the real extent of her power, Bhutto appears to have given up on all her previous ideals and simply caved in to the culture of corruption — indeed excelled in it, as she had excelled in so many other areas. In her second administration, she named her husband to multiple offices: investment minister; chief of the Intelligence Bureau; director general of the Federal Investigation Agency; chairman of the new Environment Protection Council. She and Zardari now set about seriously enriching themselves, on a scale that seems hardly credible in a country where so many people went hungry. The Pakistani economist Riaz Haq has called the 1990s "the lost decade": "In the 1990s, economic growth plummeted to between 3% and 4%, poverty rose to 33%, inflation was in double digits, and the foreign debt mounted to nearly the entire GDP of Pakistan as the governments of Benazir Bhutto (PPP) and Nawaz Sharif (PML) played musical chairs. Before Sharif was ousted in 1999, the two parties had presided over a decade of corruption and mismanagement."[7] The percentage of households living in absolute poverty doubled during that period.[8] Income inequality also increased in the 1990s, according to the Human Development in South Asia report — the worst showing of any decade between 1960 and the report's publication in 2007.

Bhutto's defenders have blamed the graft on Zardari — Mr. Ten (by now more like Twenty) Percent — and certainly he was more than provocative in his crass display of greed. But as the country's prime minister and as a wife who had been the senior partner in her marriage since the very beginning, Bhutto enabled everything Zardari did. And among the other glittering prizes she showered on him was a monopoly on Pakistan's gold imports, a post that netted him some $10 million, which he prudently deposited in a Citibank account in Dubai.

In a comprehensive piece of investigative journalism in The New York Times, the reporter John Burns compiled a mountain of damning evidence against Bhutto and Zardari, aided by documents, sold to the Times by an unnamed seller, that included Zardari's Citibank accounts in Dubai and Geneva, letters from executives offering payoffs, and paperwork incorporating the offshore companies, many in the British Virgin Islands, used as fronts for the deals.[9] Among the transactions from which Zardari skimmed off the top, the documents demonstrated, were "defense contracts; power plant projects; the privatization of state-owned industries; the awarding of broadcast licenses; the granting of an export monopoly for the country's huge rice harvest; the purchase of planes for Pakistan International Airlines; the assignment of textile export quotas; the granting of oil and gas permits; authorization to build sugar mills; and the sale of government lands."[10] The takings had been estimated at $1.5 billion as early as 1996; they grew rapidly over the next decade, until at final count Bhutto and Zardari are thought to have bilked their country of $2 billion to $3 billion.

In the meantime, they were hardly upholding their share of the country's tax burden. The highest income Bhutto declared, according to Burns's information, was $42,000 in 1996. In 1993 and 1994, during her second term as prime minister, she paid no income tax at all. "Mr. Zardari's highest declared income," Burns went on, "was $13,000, also in 1996, when interest on bank deposits he controlled in Switzerland exceeded that much every week."[11] An inquiry conducted by Pakistan's Accountability Bureau revealed that in that year, Benazir, Nusrat Bhutto, and Zardari together declared assets totaling only $1.2 million, a sum that did not include the substantial foreign accounts and properties they also held.

At the same time, Benazir's pretensions were elevated from the monarchical (the traditional Bhutto family style) to the positively imperial. In 1993 she decided to turn the family burial ground at Garhi Khuda Bakhsh near Larkana into an official mausoleum that would rival even the Taj Mahal in size and glitz, if not in beauty. To this end she sponsored an architecture competition; the first architect began work, but Bhutto sacked him when she decided she wanted the place to look more Islamic. Work would not resume until 2003, when Bhutto was out of office and had more time on her hands. She asked the new architect, Waqar Akbar Rizvi, to visit the tombs of Ayatollah Khomeini and Atatürk for inspiration, and the results were nothing if not eclectic, with Rizvi including elements of the Shalimar Gardens in his design as well. Bhutto's purpose was of course political as well as filial; she intended the mausoleum to be a national pilgrimage site, enhancing the family's already formidable *pir* status as well as her father's importance as a *shaheed*.

Edifices for the living Bhuttos kept pace with those of the dead. In addition to their other properties — their Karachi and Larkana homes, a London flat, houses in Dubai and France, and Zardari's New York apartment — Bhutto and Zardari built a new $50 million prime minister's residence on 110 acres in Islamabad, a structure later described by William Dalrymple as "a giddy, pseudo-Mexican ranch house"[12]; after they moved in, Zardari ordered 11.5 acres of protected land to be turned into his private polo center. (Not that he himself paid for any of this; instead, he diverted $1.3 million from a budget slated for public amenities.) In 1995 Zardari purchased and fixed up Rockwood, a fifteen-bedroom Surrey estate just forty minutes from London, complete with heated indoor pool and nine-hole golf course. The purchase was made through a series of companies based in the Isle of Man so as to hide evidence of ownership.[13] This property, too, Zardari intended to turn into a polo center. He filled it with rich appurtenances, including a £120,000 glass Lalique dining table, gilded furniture, and a bar that was a replica of a nearby pub, all in a garish taste that did not best please the local gentry. In this he may or may not have been abetted by his wife; in later interviews, she claimed never to have laid eyes on the place.

12

A S HER LEADERSHIP became increasingly imperial, Bhutto had become ever less popular with the average Pakistani voter. Then suddenly, at the beginning of her second term, she found herself facing opposition
within the Bhutto Family Party itself. Mir Murtaza Bhutto, as
Z. A. Bhutto's elder son, had never been happy about his sister's usurpation of leadership in the family and the party, but
he was hardly in a position to do anything about it, as the Zia
administration had filed many legal cases against him; a return
to Pakistan would inevitably mean a jail cell. For a decade he
had stayed in Syria as a guest of the Assad regime. Soon after
Shah Nawaz's death, Murtaza's marriage to Fowzia fell apart. He
won custody of his daughter, Fatima, and before long began seeing a young Lebanese exile in Damascus, Ghinwa Itaoui. The
two were married in 1989, and Ghinwa became the new mother
of Fatima as well as of the new baby she had with Murtaza —
Zulfikar Ali Bhutto II. Ghinwa was a serious young woman and
a dedicated wife and mother, though Benazir referred to her
contemptuously as a "Lebanese belly dancer."

In the summer of 1993, Murtaza decided that the time had
come for him to return to Pakistan, come what may, to face his
legal trials and stand for election to the National Assembly, running as an Independent: his sister had made it abundantly clear
that he was not welcome in her party. While it was not yet safe

for him to return to his country, Ghinwa and eleven-year-old Fatima flew there to campaign on his behalf in the October elections. (Candidates are allowed to run in absentia in Pakistan.) They were joined in their efforts by Nusrat Bhutto, who had become a passionate supporter of her son's candidacy despite the fierce resistance of Benazir, who feared, not unreasonably in patriarchal Pakistan, that Murtaza could prove a real challenge to her leadership and siphon off a critical mass of votes. Nusrat later said that she had asked Benazir to name Murtaza as chief minister of Sindh province if she was elected, and her daughter had refused outright.

Murtaza contested twenty-three seats; in the end he won only one, in the Bhutto home district of Larkana, for the provincial Sindh Assembly. He departed for Pakistan — which he had last seen sixteen years previously — on November 2, traveling in the presidential plane lent to him by Syria's president Hafiz al-Assad, but the Pakistani government denied it air clearance and it had to land in Dubai, whence Murtaza traveled to Karachi via Ethiopian Airlines. He was met by police upon arrival, arrested — there were something like ninety outstanding cases against him, amassed under Zia's regime — and taken directly to Landhi Jail, where he was held for eight months in solitary confinement.

He had, of course, expected the arrest and was prepared for the tribulations that followed. He was formally charged in six cases, all involving treason and sedition and all punishable by death. Thanks to the peculiar Pakistani legal system he was allowed to leave prison to fulfill his duties as a member of the provincial parliament. He was taken to the Sindh Assembly to be sworn in, and was also allowed to speak to the press, an opportunity he took advantage of to rail passionately against the country's culture of corruption. Murtaza's faults were only too obvious, but he appeared to be sincere in his socialist beliefs — he called for progressive taxation, even on landowners — and despite his rich-boy background he had not been tainted by financial corruption. People listened; many were attracted by his message.

Benazir, enraged by her mother's support for Murtaza, retaliated by ousting Nusrat from her ceremonial post as honorary chairperson of the PPP, with the assent of what one insider has called the party's "rubber-stamping central committee."[1] Benazir herself had been the effective ruler of the party since her arrival in England in 1984; she now made her leadership more than official by naming herself chairperson for life. This only underlined the critique her brother was aiming at the regime, for he was demanding party elections within the PPP, a move that might have toppled Benazir from power.

Nusrat openly expressed her rage with Benazir at this time. "She's talked a lot about democracy," she said angrily to the *New York Times*, "but she's become a little dictator."[2] In another interview, Nusrat said that her daughter had "definitely gone cuckoo" and was "obviously afraid of her family."[3] Nusrat's close political alliance with Benazir, in force since Zulfikar's arrest in 1977, unraveled rapidly, leading one to conjecture that Nusrat, a powerful woman in her own right and accustomed to her share of political clout, might have been chafing under Benazir's imperiousness for years. Now she complained publicly about her daughter's arrogance, even, on occasion, comparing her with the hated Zia.

Benazir decided to blame Nusrat's favoring of Murtaza on traditional Muslim sexism. "Through all this," she told *New York Times* reporter Henry Kamm, "I hoped the day would never come when I would have to battle male prejudice in my own family. It was a cruel stab in my heart when my mother declared that the male should inherit... Once my father died," she continued melodramatically, "I knew the day would come when, like all feudal families, they'd lock up the daughter so that the son takes over."[4] She also accused Nusrat of having played favorites throughout the siblings' childhood. "All my life I was such a dutiful daughter," she complained to an American journalist. "And perhaps my mother found it difficult to accept that when the time came for a decision between political responsibility and obedience as a daughter, I chose political responsibility. She's basically angry with me because she was removed as chairperson of the party. She blames me for it. But that was a party decision endorsed by a party convention of several hundred people."[5]

As was true under Zia, actions of Benazir's regime could not always be laid at her door, so she was able to disclaim personal responsibility when, in January 1994, a police cordon appeared around al-Murtaza in Larkana, preventing Nusrat and Murtaza's supporters from performing a ceremony of politically charged public prayers at Zulfikar's tomb on what would have been his sixty-sixth birthday. Gunfire was exchanged, after which at least one of Murtaza's supporters was dead (Nusrat claimed three) and several more were wounded. Ghinwa believed that Nusrat had been actively targeted. Nusrat, outraged, loudly blamed Benazir to the BBC, the Pakistani press, and the *New York Times*. Murtaza was released on bail in June; it was said by some that the army had ordered Benazir to let him out soon, lest he become a popular hero.

In the meantime, Bhutto's government was once more beset by ethnic violence in Sindh, where the MQM, representing the *muhajir* population, was inciting riots and violence to protest the government's treatment of the *muhajirs*. The fact that the MQM were political opponents of the PPP within Sindh added urgency to the conflict. In her eagerness to suppress the MQM for good, Bhutto bypassed legal channels and gave carte blanche to her interior minister, General Naseerullah Babar, who launched a brutal offensive against the MQM — an acceleration of an aggressive program originated by Nawaz Sharif, code-named Operation Clean-up or, alternatively, Operation Blue Fox.

The methods employed by Babar and his lieutenants hearkened right back to the bad old days of Zia. In January 1995, Amnesty International issued a report entitled "Pakistan: The Pattern Persists," which contrasted Bhutto and the PPP's 1993 election platform with the human rights record they had accrued in the fifteen months since taking office. The manifesto had pledged that under PPP rule discriminatory laws would end, loss of life at the hands of state authorities would be subject to judicial review, torture and every form of human degradation would be banned, and citizens would not be hauled up before the police without evidence. But almost immediately, the report noted, "the new government failed to give a strong and clear public signal that everyone responsible for human rights violations would be brought to justice," and "even criminals with public records are appointed as long as their political loyalties suit the powers that be." Torture continued to be "widespread and systematic" in Pakistani prisons, with suspects being hung upside down and beaten with *sachoos* (paddles containing sharp nails to tear flesh), given electric shocks, even having holes drilled into their bodies. Custodial rape was frequent, as were extrajudicial killings and "disappearings." "Torture was applied in Pakistan in the first 15 months of PPP government to criminal suspects, political opponents and ordinary citizens equally. Torture was used to gain information, to punish, humiliate or intimidate, to take revenge and — most often — to extract money." Violators of human rights abuse laws were given "virtual impunity" by the authorities.[6]

By the time Operation Clean-up was declared complete, there were some three thousand official dead in Karachi; true numbers are probably far higher. Murtaza continued to use his prominent position to call attention to the rot inside the PPP, and in March 1995 he launched a spin-off of the party that he provocatively named the PPP (Shaheed Bhutto) — thus implying that his own program and philosophy cohered more closely to the family *shaheed*'s than did those of his errant sister Benazir, to whom he now referred as "Begum Zardari," as if she should no longer be considered a Bhutto at all. The new party's manifesto, written by Murtaza himself, displayed a combination of earnest naïveté and hero worship of the flawed patriarch.

Any love that had once existed between Benazir and Murtaza was now long gone: their hostility was mutual and implacable, and Murtaza made manifest his contempt for the patently corrupt Zardari time and again. Now master of 70 Clifton, Murtaza hung Zardari's portrait in the guest lavatory; he is even said to have shaved off half his brother-in-law's luxuriant moustache in a not-so-friendly bit of roughhousing. According to one report, Murtaza's guards aimed automatic weapons at Zardari from a passing vehicle on the airport highway in a blatant attempt at intimidation.

At 7:30 in the evening on September 20, 1996, Murtaza was approaching 70 Clifton with his entourage, in a convoy of four vehicles. As he neared the house the group noted that the streetlights throughout Clifton had been turned off; the neighborhood was dark and thronged with silent police officers, estimated at numbering between seventy and one hundred. Snipers were visible, positioned in treetops. Murtaza, who immediately understood what was happening, got out of the car with his hands up. The police opened fire gangland style, killing seven people. Murtaza was hit at close range and died later at the hospital.

The operation was characteristic of the so-called encounter killings that had been occurring throughout recent Pakistani history: extrajudicial executions carried out by the police, made to look as if they were armed clashes between rival gangs. Ghinwa and the fourteen-year-old Fatima, who had been inside the house awaiting Murtaza's return, heard nothing until it was all over. By the time they got wind of the tragedy and rushed into the street, around 8:45 p.m., all evidence had been cleared away and the street had been hosed down. "It was standard Operation Clean-Up," Fatima Bhutto later wrote: "keep the bodies, destroy the evidence."[7] "The trap had carefully been laid," commented Tariq Ali,

> but as is the way in Pakistan, the crudeness of the operation — false entries in police logbooks, lost evidence, witnesses arrested and intimidated, the provincial PPP governor (regarded as untrustworthy) dispatched to a nonevent in Egypt, a policeman killed who was feared might talk — made it obvious that the decision to execute the prime minister's brother had been made at a high level. Shoaib Suddle, deputy inspector general of Sind when Murtaza was murdered, was charged with involvement in the killing, but the case was dismissed before it went to trial. He was subsequently promoted to inspector general by Zardari in April 2008. Two months later, he was appointed director general of the Intelligence Bureau in Islamabad.[8]

As Pakistan expert Owen Bennett-Jones has written, "The Pakistani police rarely know whether their political masters want an investigation or not. As a general rule they assume the politicians are hoping for a cover-up and actively investigate only when specifically ordered to do so."[9] All the survivors from the convoy, and all witnesses to Murtaza's murder, were taken into police custody. Two died there; the rest were not released until three months later, after Bhutto's government had fallen. A few days after the killing, the station house officer of the Clifton police force died under mysterious circumstances; his widow claimed she had seen two men running from the scene.

Bhutto, tearful, blamed the whole nightmare on a conspiracy against the Bhutto family, and her administration set up a tribunal, headed by a Supreme Court judge, to look into the assassination. Murtaza's lawyers directly accused Asif Ali Zardari of conspiracy to murder, along with the chief minister of Sindh, Abdullah Shah, and two police officials. The tribunal denied that there was any legal evidence linking Zardari to the murder but admitted that the hit was an extrajudicial killing by the police and that it could not have been pulled off without approval at a very high level. Bhutto, by then out of power again, tried to lay the blame at the door of President Farooq Leghari, but no one took this allegation seriously.

Was Zardari responsible for this crime, as many have believed? More important, was Bhutto herself guilty, if only of sitting back and letting it happen? There is no question but that Murtaza constituted a considerable threat to her political life. Even had she been able to successfully keep him out of power, her behavior toward him would have harmed her politically: an older sister ruthlessly defending her place atop the heap was not the loving family woman the public wanted to look up to. Already, unsympathetic Pakistanis had been comparing her with Aurangzeb, the seventeenth-century Mughal prince who had brutally defeated his three brothers in a battle to succeed their father as emperor.

Murtaza's supporters within the PPP, in any case, connected not only Zardari but Bhutto, too, with the murder. When she tried to attend Murtaza's funeral at Larkana, local PPP (Shaheed Bhutto) supporters pelted her car with stones. And at the funeral itself, Nusrat, now in the early stages of Alzheimer's disease, also blamed Benazir for the death of her brother. In 2010, after her aunt's death, Fatima Bhutto would make her suspicions more explicit, pointedly failing to differentiate between the will of Zardari and that of her aunt Benazir. Benazir's attitude to Murtaza, some have suggested, was rather like that of King Henry II regarding Thomas à Becket: "Will no one rid me of this troublesome priest?"

WHATEVER THE FIRST Couple's involvement in this murder might have been, Murtaza's death served as a convenient excuse to get rid of them, and in November 1996 President Farooq Leghari, so long a complaisant servant of the Bhutto regime, dismissed the prime minister on charges of corruption and suspicion of involvement in her brother's death, again citing the Eighth Amendment. Bhutto immediately challenged the constitutionality of the decision, but the Supreme Court upheld Leghari, who took the opportunity of the moment to also dismiss all pro-Bhutto elements in the military leadership.

Zardari was in even hotter water than his wife, for his involvement in Murtaza's death seemed very probable. He decided to make his way to safety in Dubai, but he was arrested in Lahore while on his way out of the country and taken to jail on charges of money laundering and murder. He would remain in prison until late in 2004.

A woman of lesser mettle than Bhutto might now have retreated to safety and peace in Dubai or London, but she stayed on and contested the general election later that year. Predictably, the PPP was defeated and Nawaz Sharif was prime minister once again. As tireless leader of the opposition, Bhutto functioned as his chief gadfly during his time in office.

Sharif's new term was to be no easier than Bhutto's had

been. In September 1996 the Taliban finally took power in Afghanistan; years of fighting had left the country devastated and its capital, Kabul, a pile of rubble. Pakistan recognized the Taliban as Afghanistan's legitimate government, one of only three countries in the world to do so, in a move that further isolated the country from its allies and supporters in the West. It would not be not be until 2001 and the War on Terror that Pakistan would once more find a genuinely enthusiastic sponsor in the United States.

And then India detonated a nuclear bomb in 1998, causing a nasty shock in Islamabad. Bhutto's reaction was astonishing, considering her carefully groomed image as a levelheaded leader who favored diplomacy over saber rattling, and her previous assurances to her American military sponsors that her government was not developing a bomb: she now tried desperately to drum up rage against India from the international community. An incendiary editorial she wrote for the *Los Angeles Times* shockingly called for a preemptive strike. "While the world slept," she began the piece in high Churchillian manner, "India detonated a series of nuclear tests signaling its determination to threaten the entire nonproliferation regime in the region . . . I am not a military expert. But I believe that sanctions simply are not enough. Rogue nations that try to defy world opinion ought to be taught a lesson. If a preemptive military strike is possible to neutralize India's nuclear capability, that is the response that is necessary."[1] She also challenged the Sharif administration to retaliate aggressively with nuclear tests of its own. Emily MacFarquhar, a journalist investigating Bhutto at this time, described the scene: "Theatrically tossing glass bangles on the ground, she taunted Prime Minister Nawaz Sharif as a womanly wimp for not rushing to test."[2]

Sharif did indeed detonate a Pakistani bomb, and with her country's face now saved, Bhutto returned to a stance of statesmanlike dignity and called for Pakistan to sign the Comprehensive Nuclear Test-Ban Treaty and come to a bilateral agreement with India as well. A month later, four Pakistani nuclear scientists fled the country, claiming that they had been given orders to provide data for possible nuclear strikes against India. Bhutto now reverted to silence on the subject.

The career of rising military officer Pervez Musharraf had flourished under both Bhutto and Sharif. He had been a key member of Bhutto's staff, particularly in her second administration, and, with her blessing, had assisted the ISI in supporting the rise of the Taliban. Now Sharif appointed him chairman of the Joint Chiefs of Staff—a choice that would prove nearly as disastrous as Z. A. Bhutto's selection of Zia.

It was probably under Musharraf's direction that Pakistan unwisely involved itself in the Kargil War of 1999, yet another conflagration along the Pakistani-Kashmiri Line of Control. In April, Kashmiri guerrillas captured posts along the line and launched an artillery attack on the highway running north from Srinagar. Pakistan claimed to have had nothing to do with the guerrillas' actions, but India determined—correctly, as it turned out—that the guerrillas were really members of Pakistan's Northern Light Infantry. As the two sides continued fighting, escalation into nuclear war seemed very possible; bowing to pressure from American president Bill Clinton, Pakistan ceased hostilities and used its influence to have the guerrillas refrain from further aggression. By the end of the war, as many as four thousand people were dead.

Bhutto pressed for an investigation into the events leading to the Kargil disaster, claiming that during her second term Musharraf had presented her with a war games scenario that was exactly that of the Kargil offensive; she had told him in no uncertain terms, she said, that the plan was not only morally wrong but unworkable. She also used the opportunity to rail against the generals once more, accusing them of financial corruption as well as despotism; the generals, she cried, felt no compunction in investigating politicians, but no one had the authority to investigate *them* for the selfsame crimes.

Sure enough, in April, law enforcement closed in on Bhutto as it had done on her husband. She was sentenced to five years in jail, banned from politics for five years, and asked to repay $8.6 million to the Pakistani government. She was staying in London when the conviction came through, and rather than return to Pakistan she fled to Dubai. With her went Bilawal, eleven, and the younger Zardari children, two daughters named Bakhtawar and Aseefa, now nine and six years old, respectively. From Dubai Bhutto expressed concerns about returning home: "If the Supreme Court rejects my appeal, I fear I will be murdered in jail." A not unreasonable fear, considering the family history.

The Dubai bolthole had been decades in the preparation. Sheikh Zayed bin Sultan Al Nahyan, president of the United Arab Emirates, had been sedulously courted by Z. A. Bhutto, who had granted this fabulously rich and powerful man a little fiefdom of his own within Pakistan: a hunting lodge with a private airstrip, the services of the local police and civil service, and exemption from local laws and customs inspections. Upon Zulfikar's death, Sheikh Zayed informed Nusrat that he considered the Bhuttos a part of his family. From then on they enjoyed free accommodations in UAE, all expenses paid, under the sole condition that they made no mention of their location to the press. Now Bhutto and her children took up residence in a splendiferous pink villa in Dubai's Emirates Hills, as guests of the regime. She would stay there for eight years, during five of which Asif remained jailed in Pakistan without trial.

Mr. and Mrs. Ten Percent were now in trouble in Europe as well as Pakistan, pursued by nemesis in the form of a relentless Swiss magistrate, Daniel Devaud. In 1998 Devaud had seized from a safe-deposit box a $190,000 sapphire-and-diamond necklace Bhutto had purchased on Bond Street the previous year; this launched what would turn into a six-year investigation into the sources of the money that was used to pay for this bauble. A BBC investigation led by Owen Bennett-Jones followed Devaud's research. The magistrate's investigations uncovered a plethora of dirty deals, including an agreement in which Dassault Aviation in France agreed to pay Zardari and a Pakistani partner $200 million to okay a $4 billion jet fighter sale, and another in which a Swiss firm hired to prevent customs fraud in Pakistan shelled out millions to offshore companies controlled by Zardari and, at least on paper, by Nusrat Bhutto.

In 2004 an English court would render a decision that the Rockwood estate should be sold and the proceeds returned to the government of Pakistan, the rightful owner of the property. Up to this point Zardari had not admitted he had anything to do with Rockwood: "How can anyone think of buying a mansion in England," he asked reporters, "when people in Pakistan don't even have a roof over their heads?"[3] Now he demanded that he, as the rightful owner, receive the proceeds from the sale. Workmen, angry at not having been paid, squatted for months in the corridors of Rockwood, alarming its new owners.[4]

How culpable was Bhutto in all of this, aside from her Marie Antoinette–scale spending (the role of a diamond necklace in the downfalls of both women is a striking coincidence) and her actions in giving her husband high office and turning a blind eye to his obvious thefts? Najam Sethi, who led the Pakistani corruption investigation, said that Bhutto and Zardari had affixed yellow Post-it notes to particular files to indicate favors and deals and that these notes were carefully removed after the completion of each deal. It's not that Bhutto's fingerprints weren't on the deals; it's just that they were very carefully removed.

In the end, Devaud concluded that Bhutto was indeed guilty of criminal actions, specifically in the SGS/Cotecna deal in which she and Zardari were convicted of taking approximately $15 million in exchange for awarding the customs contract to these Swiss firms, abetted by a Swiss lawyer who had been the Bhutto family's financial adviser for several years, Jens Schlegelmilch. Devaud found Zardari and Bhutto equally guilty of money laundering and receiving kickbacks, with Benazir controlling key bank accounts. "Benazir Bhutto," he wrote when he rendered his decision, "knew she was acting in a criminally reprehensible manner by abusing her role in order to obtain for herself and for her husband considerable sums in the interest of her family at the cost of the Islamic Republic of Pakistan."[5] Bhutto and Zardari were ordered to turn over $11.9 million in kickbacks, as well as the necklace, to the government of Pakistan, and to serve 180 days in prison. Seventeen Swiss bank accounts belonging to the Bhutto-Zardari family were frozen.

Bhutto's reaction to these devastating allegations was defensive and yet characteristically high-handed: her spokesman called the investigation a witch hunt and likened it to McCarthyism. Bhutto herself accused Devaud of character assassination and wondered aloud why there was so much fuss over her high-spending ways. "I mean, what is poor and what is rich?" she demanded. "If you mean, am I rich by European standards, do I have a billion dollars, or even a hundred million dollars, even half that, no, I do not. But if you mean that I'm ordinary rich, yes, my father had three children studying at Harvard as undergraduates at the same time. But this wealth never meant anything to my brothers or me."[6] It was not for nothing that Jemima Goldsmith Khan, wife of Bhutto's political rival Imran Khan, dubbed Benazir a kleptocrat in an Hermès headscarf, and that in 1996, after three years of Bhutto rule, Transparency International declared Pakistan the second most corrupt country in the world. Even Husain Haqqani, who had served loyally as Bhutto's press secretary, expressed his disgust: "She no longer made the distinction between the Bhuttos and Pakistan. In her mind, she was Pakistan, so she could do as she pleased."[7]

Bhutto never served the sentence, and she ignored the summons from the Swiss court, challenging the verdict and securing a retrial. In February 2001, the *Sunday Times* of London printed transcripts of some tapped phone conversations that suggested that the Sharif regime had put pressure on the judge to convict Bhutto and Zardari and pass a heavy sentence, and the verdict was overturned, but no one seriously suggested that the evidence had been fixed or that Bhutto and Zardari were not thieves on a grand scale.

In 1999, Nawaz Sharif made a fateful move when he announced his decision to replace army chief Pervez Musharraf with a rival officer. The military mobilized behind Musharraf; when Sharif attempted to keep the general from landing at the Karachi airport (he was returning from a trip to Sri Lanka) and to divert his plane to India, soldiers surrounded the air traffic control tower and cleared the way for the plane to land. Sharif was placed under arrest. Pakistan's Supreme Court validated the coup, and Musharraf ascended to the presidency.

Nawaz Sharif might very well have gone the way of Z. A. Bhutto. He had been arrested on charges of hijacking, kidnapping, attempted murder, and treason for trying to prevent Musharraf's landing at the Karachi airport. He was placed in the same jail that had housed Bhutto, and the leader of his defense team was assassinated in the streets of Karachi. Had it not been for the pressure applied by Bill Clinton and King Fahd of Saudi Arabia, Sharif's trial might have been as outrageous a farce as Bhutto's had been. Indeed, it looked as if that was the way it was heading, for Sharif was rapidly convicted and a death sentence was expected. Instead, Sharif was released to exile in Saudi Arabia in 2000, on the condition that he not seek public office in Pakistan for the next twenty-one years. Benazir Bhutto, who one would have thought would have been horrified by this repetition of the traumatic events of 1977, is reported to have celebrated her rival's fall by distributing sweets.

For all the fundamental differences between the Bhutto and Sharif governments, Owen Bennett-Jones has noted, the similarities were striking. "Neither pushed through any significant reforms," he pointed out:

> In national policy terms, their most important shared characteristic was their ability to run up huge levels of foreign debt. By the time General Musharraf took over in 1999, Pakistan owed foreign creditors over $25 billion and debt servicing had become the largest component of the annual budget. Most of the debt had been run up in the 1990s... General Zia, and to a lesser extent Zulfikar Ali Bhutto, may have been profligate but their appetite for foreign loans was dwarfed by that of Nawaz Sharif and Benazir Bhutto.[8]

By contrast, Pervez Musharraf turned out to be a rather effective administrator. In the first few years of his rule, the nation saw economic growth of about 8 percent, a well-performing stock market, freer media, and a boom for the middle class. He was also a committed secularist and succeeded in making a major step that Bhutto had never dared try: the repeal of the Hudood Ordinances.

The coup had been condemned roundly by the international community, but all was to change on September 11, 2001. Musharraf's agreement to join the War on Terror once more made Pakistan America's favorite client state and Musharraf our kind of dictator; at that moment in history, the United States would hardly have supported a return to democracy in Pakistan even under its erstwhile friend Benazir Bhutto. Musharraf consolidated his political gains by amending the constitution to ban prime ministers from serving more than two terms in office: this knocked both Bhutto and Sharif out of the political game for the foreseeable future, or at least until the constitution might be altered again. He also held a national referendum to affirm his presidency for another five years.

From Dubai, where she lived from 1999 to 2007, Bhutto watched the events in Pakistan impatiently. A political animal to her core, she must have found the enforced distance from the action deeply frustrating, though she did her best to run the PPP in absentia. She was still a player in Pakistani politics, but for a masterly hands-on politician, life without the crowds, the chanting, the electrifying communion between herself and her supporters must have seemed thin indeed. Bhutto's choice of Dubai rather than England as a place of exile was due to its proximity to Pakistan: everyone traveling between Pakistan and the West had to stop over in Dubai, and thus she was able to keep abreast of events at home and play her role in them, however diminished it might have become. With time on her hands, she occupied herself with domestic tasks. Not that she had to do housework in the pink villa; there were plenty of servants. But she had three children to raise and the care of Nusrat, whose Alzheimer's disease had progressed to the point where she was unable to speak, recognize family members, or tend to her own needs in any way: dressed in white, she wandered ghostlike through the house, and in and out of the servants' quarters. "I find this taking care of her very painful," Bhutto told Amy Wilentz. "I remember my mother being glamorous and well-dressed and you know, so confident."[9]

Even the ebullient, self-assured Bhutto sometimes found it hard to keep gloom at bay. She missed her country and her place in it; her life was rather lonely, her family sadly dwindled: "The Bhutto family doesn't exist any longer. My family, the Bhutto family, doesn't exist; my mother is sick, my two brothers are gone, my sister's leading a quiet life far away."[10] Zardari languished in prison until 2004, developing diabetes and a heart condition. When he was finally released he went to New

York for medical treatment, after which he opted to stay on in his New York apartment with his dogs rather than return to his family in Dubai; the three children flew to America on holidays to visit him. Whether this was his own decision or his wife's has never been clear. While the couple did not officially announce that they were separated, it was evident that this was the case, though Bhutto, who was still head of the PPP and had not ruled out a return to active politics, could not publicly admit to a rift with her husband.

By this time she had aged and put on weight, but her charisma appeared undiminished — even enhanced, perhaps, as the years went on. Rory McCarthy, a British journalist who was sent to interview her, found her — to his surprise — "immediately charming."

> Flirtatious, funny, questioning and eager to listen, she spends her conversations continually and self-consciously adjusting the translucent white dupatta covering her long, thick hair ... Few Pakistani politicians truly enjoy engaging with their crowds of supporters and rarely give more than a brisk wave from inside their expensive, air-conditioned four-wheel drives. Bhutto has a much more refined political touch and always delights in meeting the people who have come out to support her, frequently singling out the women in particular. It is this effusive but innate charm which has created for her such a reputation.[11]

She stood on her dignity when McCarthy said that the only reason he could find for her contemplating a return to Pakistan was that she was addicted to power. "Whatever my aims and agendas were," she replied, not entirely truthfully, "I never asked for power. I think they need me. I don't think it's addictive, I think, if anything, it's the opposite of addictive. You want to run away from it, but it doesn't let you go. It's doing it again."[12]

14

BHUTTO AND NAWAZ Sharif were now in the same boat: both in exile, both wishing to return to power. Neither of them had a hope of this outcome unless Pakistan was returned to at least nominal democratic rule. Could it happen? Musharraf, an efficient if not an inspirational leader, was now floundering. Since September 11, 2001, he had been one of the mainstays of the US War on Terror, in Washington's eyes as indispensable a bulwark against the forces of Evil as Zia had been during the 1980s. Although he had taken power in an antidemocratic military coup, the George W. Bush administration floated him with oceans of cash: a 45,000 percent increase in military aid, according to Britain's *Guardian,* totaling some $4 billion.[1]

But in Washington's eyes Musharraf had never played a straight game. He had accepted American money and pledged to help his benefactors while refraining from cracking down on *jihadi* groups and terrorist plotters, especially in the North-West Frontier Province. There were still thousands of unregulated madrasas throughout Pakistan, in spite of the fact that the United States had repeatedly requested that Musharraf keep an eye on their doings. On top of this, the support he did supply the United States was making Musharraf increasingly unpopular with Pakistanis, who resented the continuance of military rule. Human rights violations by out-of-control security forces were becoming an international disgrace.

Sensing a new vulnerability in their common foe, Bhutto

and Sharif, who had cordially detested each other for years, came to the conclusion that if they united they might just have a chance to bring Musharraf down. In May 2006 they met in London (they both maintained homes there) and signed a document they called the Charter of Democracy, calling for an end to military rule and setting out a list of conditions they believed should be met by responsible government. The two ex–prime ministers stopped sniping at each other in public and valiantly maintained a show of solidarity. And this, it must be said, was a remarkable change in its own right.

What Bhutto and Sharif wanted was power, and the sooner they got it, the better. What Washington wanted was a continuation of the sort of military, authoritarian regime in Pakistan that the United States had grown comfortable manipulating from afar, but with a facade of democracy that the White House, Pentagon, and CIA felt could best be provided by Bhutto. It's true that after so many years of overexposure, the image of the wholesome Ivy League coed was beginning to wear a little thin. But the American public still saw her as progressive and reform-minded — still "one of us."

Thus began the deal brokered by Washington and submitted to by Bhutto and Musharraf, a deal cynics likened to an arranged marriage. "The couple's distaste for each other yielded to a mutual dependence on the United States," commented Tariq Ali.[2] The Pakistani media demonstrated its displeasure with Washington's political solution, but "a whitewashed Benazir Bhutto was presented on U.S. networks and BBC TV news as 'the former prime minister' rather than the fugitive politician facing corruption charges in several countries."[3]

Bhutto had been considered a nonperson by the Bush administration, which was intent on building up Musharraf's image. Now the Americans did their best to restore a little of the sheen of 1988. During the course of 2007 she was brought to the States for a series of meetings with American power brokers, including Secretary of State Condoleezza Rice's senior deputies Richard Boucher and Nicholas Burns and the US ambassador to the UN, Zalmay Khalilzad. She and Mark Siegel collaborated on *Reconciliation,* an anodyne, politically correct treatise detailing the common interests of Muslims and Westerners.

The corruption charges, in any case, were disposed of relatively easily once Bhutto had demonstrated that she was ready to play ball with Washington. Bhutto and Musharraf met secretly in Abu Dhabi, under American auspices; there the general paved the way for the prodigal daughter's return to Pakistan — and for that of Sharif as well — by having a legal ruling drawn up that nullified all pending criminal cases against politicians, a measure euphemistically named the National Reconciliation Ordinance. (England and Spain, in a solidarity gesture clearly aimed at the United States, also canceled pending cases against Bhutto, though Switzerland stood its ground and declined to do so.) In addition, the National Reconciliation Ordinance erased the inconvenient constitutional clause, introduced by Musharraf, forbidding any politician to serve more than two terms as prime minister.

In return for this clemency Bhutto had to agree to support Musharraf's candidacy as a civilian president and to ask her supporters in the PPP not to vote against him in the forthcoming election that would confirm his presidency for another five years. But Bhutto insisted that Musharraf resign as military chief, so that at least a facade of civilian rule might be maintained. "We do not accept President Musharraf in uniform," she told the press. "Our stand is that. I stick to my stand."[4] Musharraf, she said, should seek reelection as president after the elections for the National Assembly took place in November, and he must stand as a civilian. When pressed, she refused to rule out the possibility that as prime minister she might award her errant husband a government post in a new Bhutto administration.

When the terms of the "arranged marriage" became clear to the Pakistani electorate, widespread disillusion set in. Here was no true democracy but the kind of backroom horse-trading that rendered elections meaningless. Opinion polls showed Nawaz Sharif as far ahead of Bhutto in the polls — even at a distance, exiled in Saudi Arabia — probably because he had refrained from dealing with Musharraf and the mistrusted Americans. Fatima Bhutto, who had grown into a sharp and articulate young woman and a tireless public gadfly to her aunt, wrote an editorial in the *Los Angeles Times* in which she objected passionately to Bhutto's pretensions to progressive democracy.

> Ms. Bhutto's repeated promises to end fundamentalism and terrorism in Pakistan strain credulity because, after all, the Taliban government that ran Afghanistan was recognized by Pakistan under her last government — making Pakistan one of only three governments to do so . . .
>
> Since Musharraf seized power in 1999, there has been an earnest grass-roots movement for democratic reform. The last thing we need is to be tied to a neocon agenda through a puppet "democrat" like Ms. Bhutto.
>
> By supporting Ms. Bhutto, who talks of democracy while asking to be brought to power by a military dictator, the only thing that will be accomplished is the death of the nascent secular democratic movement in my country.[5]

Things continued to go badly for Musharraf. In March, he sacked the chief justice of the Supreme Court, Iftikhar Muhammad Chaudhry — a major mistake, as it turned out. The two men had been at loggerheads for some time. Chaudhry had challenged Musharraf's acting as both president and army chief, and he had openly complained about people disappearing in government custody and the lack of due process in arrests, calling for the police to release prisoners who had not received a trial. When Musharraf dismissed Chaudhry the latter protested loudly, initiating a mass insurrection among Pakistan's legal profession. Some eighty thousand lawyers from various political parties aligned to campaign for judicial independence and to demand the reinstatement of Chaudhry. They called their action the Save the Judiciary Movement; it would become known throughout the country and beyond as the Lawyers' Movement. The lawyers organized protests and nonviolent rallies across the country. On July 20, Musharraf caved in and reinstated Chaudhry, very reluctantly.

That same month another serious crisis erupted when the pro-Taliban militants who ran the Lal Masjid (Red Mosque) in Islamabad revealed they had stockpiled large quantities of ammunition in the building. They called for the overthrow of Musharraf, who had given the hated George W. Bush so much help in the War on Terror. Clashes broke out between the students in the mosque and the police, culminating in a siege and then an assault by the military; 102 people, on both sides of the fight, were killed.

The time seemed ever riper for Bhutto's return, but Musharraf was not eager to have her on the scene; he clearly felt unequal to coping with the political excitement her arrival would probably arouse. He was even vaguely threatening about what might happen to her if she returned to Pakistan ahead of schedule: "Your security," he warned her rather ominously, "is based on the state of our relationship."[6]

When, against this advice, she did decide that she would return to Pakistan early in order to campaign on home turf, the US government also declined to be responsible for her security (a penny-wise, pound-foolish failure to protect their investment, one might say), simply recommending various contractors to her. Blackwater offered its services at a price of $400,000 per month. Bhutto declined the favor, asking Vice President Dick Cheney to hold Musharraf personally responsible for her safety and requesting that British foreign secretary David Miliband pressure Musharraf to remove several individuals in his administration whom she suspected of wishing to harm her. This request, too, was ignored.

Mark Siegel, Bhutto's publicist, as assiduous after her death as he was during her life (Zardari took him on as the official lobbyist for Pakistan, a job for which Siegel's firm was paid $1 million a year), gave the official version of Bhutto's return in his epilogue to her autobiography, written soon after her death:

> Why did Benazir proceed even though Musharraf was doing little to protect her? Her own words speak for themselves: "Some people might not understand what drives me forward into this uncharted and potentially dangerous crossroads of my life. Too many people have sacrificed too much, too many have died, and too many see me as their remaining hope for liberty, for me to stop fighting now." When Benazir touched down on Pakistan soil after eight years of exile, her countrymen and -women greeted her with a tumultuous, unprecedented show of support.[7]

Siegel estimated that up to three million Pakistanis assembled at the airport in Karachi to greet her. Not everyone agrees with his numbers. Isambard Wilkinson, the Karachi correspondent for the *Telegraph* at the time, estimated the turnout at 150,000 and described the homecoming as "orchestrated," the crowds largely made up of impoverished Pakistanis who had been "ferried in from villages" and were "awaiting their turn to perform the serfs' welcome for the great leader." "The poor," he wrote, "performed the jelsa, or political rally, with great aplomb, dancing and singing, some smoking hash and tippling on caustic homebrew." Wilkinson described the self-possessed Bhutto as looking "every inch the iconic leader of a modern Muslim nation" as she lifted her hands in prayer, a Koran dangling over-head. "The third coming of Pakistan's empress was facilitated by a large converted sea-container borne on a truck bedecked like a large howdah on a medieval elephant of war."[8]

Her convoy made its way slowly through the pressing crowds, toward Jinnah's mausoleum, where she was to make a speech. Eight hours after leaving the airport they had not yet arrived, and Bhutto, exhausted from standing for so long, descended for a moment into a cubicle inside the vehicle. At this instant, two bombs went off in a double suicide attack: 149 people were dead, 402 wounded, including many who had formed a human shield around Bhutto's truck — a special force of volunteers organized by Zardari, called the Jaan Nisarane Benazir, "those willing to die for Benazir." One of the dead was a baby in whose clothes one of the bombers had apparently stashed explosives. Bhutto herself emerged unscathed.

Enraged by the inadequate police protection and the usual official inability, or unwillingness, to get to the bottom of the crime, she filed a complaint against the government. Though she did not actually name Hamid Gul, or senior intelligence officer Ijaz Shah, or Chaudhry Pervaiz Elahi, chief minister of the Punjab and an ally of Musharraf, her friends knew that she was suspicious of these men. She requested that Musharraf call in the FBI or Scotland Yard, but he refused.

On November 1 Bhutto returned to Dubai, ostensibly to visit her family. There was open speculation that Musharraf might impose a state of emergency in her absence, especially if the Supreme Court found that his recent win in the presidential referendum was unconstitutional; opposition leaders claimed that his failure to resign from his position as army chief before the referendum rendered him ineligible. This ruling did indeed come to pass, immediately after her departure, and on November 3 Musharraf declared the expected state of emergency and suspended the 1973 constitution, claiming that such actions were necessary to keep the country from descending into chaos before the parliamentary elections. He also arrested the members of the judiciary who had ruled against the imposition of emergency measures, including Chief Justice Chaudhry, whom he placed under house arrest, incommunicado, behind barbed wire barricades, guarded by a phalanx of riot police who made sure he stayed put.

Bhutto was uncertain whether a speedy return to Pakistan was wise, but her advisers urged her to get back as quickly as possible, considering the rate at which events were moving. Upon her arrival she was immediately (and predictably) placed under house arrest before she could lead a planned rally against the state of emergency, which she described as martial law without the label. She eagerly addressed the international press, stating her pessimism about any possible power-sharing deal as long as Musharraf refused to lift the emergency and saying the PPP would probably boycott the January elections. Musharraf seemed ready to keep her in custody indefinitely, but then there came a surprise visit from US deputy secretary of state John Negroponte, who was determined to yoke Musharraf and Bhutto together, by main force if necessary. Bhutto was released from house arrest, lest the proposed "arranged marriage" look doomed from the start.

Musharraf, more tractable now, installed a caretaker government that he claimed would guide the country through the January elections; it was led by one of his own loyalists, Mohammed Mian Soomro. Musharraf now self-righteously defended his "democratic" credentials: "I take pride in the fact that, being a man in uniform, I have actually introduced the essence of democracy in Pakistan, whether anyone believes it or not," he insisted.[9]

On November 26, Nawaz Sharif returned to Pakistan after seven years in exile as the guest of King Abdullah of Saudi Arabia. He had attempted to return two months earlier but had been immediately deported again. Now, thanks perhaps to American pressure on Musharraf to make gestures toward democratic pluralism, his arrival went unimpeded. "We want democracy and nothing else," Sharif assured the BBC on his arrival in Lahore. "I am here to play my role and also make my own efforts to rid the country of dictatorship."[10] The same day, Bhutto filed nomination papers in the Larkana district for two seats in the upcoming elections. The PPP platform, she announced, would center around the Five E's: Employment, Education, Energy, Environment, Equality. She seemed no more likely to achieve significant headway on any of these problems this time than she had done during her previous terms.

Musharraf resigned as head of the military on November 28 and was sworn in as Pakistan's civilian president two days later. Bhutto and Sharif, those most uneasy allies, joined forces to demand an end to emergency rule.

15

ON DECEMBER 27, 2007, just ten days before the scheduled elections, Bhutto addressed a crowd of ten thousand at Liaquat Bagh in Rawalpindi, the site of Liaquat Ali Khan's murder in 1951 and very close to the jail where Zulfikar Ali Bhutto had been executed. After leaving the platform she returned to her armor-plated Toyota Land Cruiser. Against the advice of her security team, and with the same joy in communing with the crowd that Mary Ellen Mark had noted twenty years previously, she rose so that her head and torso appeared through the escape hatch. As she waved at the crowds there approached a gunman — later identified as a Pashtun boy named Bilal, alias Saeed, of about fifteen — who fired three shots in the space of a second. After the second, Bhutto fell "like a stone" back down through the hatch.[1] Quickly after that the boy set off a suicide bomb.

All this was determined by the later examination of mobile phone images from the event; at the time it was not clear to eyewitnesses whether Bhutto had been killed by a bullet or a bomb. Even those inside the van, a group that included PPP vice president Makhdoom Amin Fahim, a senior PPP member, and PPP political adviser Safdar Abbasi, were shaky on their stories.

Bhutto was taken to the Rawalpindi hospital, where doctors tried unsuccessfully to resuscitate her. She was declared dead at 6:16 p.m. No autopsy was performed, under express instructions from the police; later, the hospital offered the widower, Zardari, the possibility of one, but rather surprisingly, he said it was not necessary. Immediately after the attack, the scene of the assassination was washed down with a high-pressure fire hose. A spokesman for the Ministry of the Interior reported that Bhutto had died of a head injury sustained on a lever attached to the escape hatch of her vehicle.

Whether Bhutto died from a bullet or a head injury is not as important a question as just who "Bilal" was, and who had masterminded his attack. The Ministry of the Interior claimed that a tribal leader from the northwest, one Baitullah Mehsud, had ordered the assassination with support from al-Qaida — though Mehsud, through a spokesman, immediately denied responsibility. Cell phone footage shows Bhutto's chief bodyguard, Khalid Shahenshah, looking at her and running his fingers across his throat; several months later, he was mysteriously murdered. In general, the Western media was ready to blame al-Qaida and other terrorist organizations for Bhutto's death, while Pakistanis tended to believe it was an inside job, planned by Musharraf, the army, the ISI, or some coalition thereof. These players had certainly been guilty by omission, even if they had played no active role in the crime; the security they had offered Bhutto had been scandalously inadequate.

Musharraf, unhappy at being suspected of ordering Bhutto's death, asked Scotland Yard to investigate the murder, but so many obstacles were put in its way that its final report could only be inconclusive. Later, Chilean diplomat Heraldo Muñoz was delegated by UN Secretary-General Ban Ki-moon to lead an investigation. He gave the details of the killing and its aftermath in his report to the UN, later expanded and published as a book, *Getting Away with Murder: Benazir Bhutto's Assassination and the Politics of Pakistan*. The quick cleanup, the police's refusal to allow the hospital to perform an autopsy, and other indicators made it clear that some sort of cover-up was in play.

People in the government and military were visibly nervous about talking to the UN team. Hamid Gul absolutely refused to do so. Cell phone footage seen by the team demonstrated not only that Bhutto had received minimal police protection but also that the police might well have been actively involved in the deed. Evidence collected was minimal and not of much use. The Land Cruiser had been carefully cleaned and scrubbed by the police while the investigation was still under way.

"It is my belief that the police deliberately botched the investigation into Bhutto's assassination," Muñoz asserted, unsurprisingly[2]—but why, and were they alone? Was the ISI involved, as seemed probable to most who speculated on the case? Muñoz was convinced "that Police Chief Saud Aziz did not act independently in deciding to hose down the crime scene . . . The only precedents for hosing down a crime scene involved military targets. [He does not mention Murtaza's murder.] Some police officials saw this as further indication that the military was involved."[3] Many, including the powers-that-be in Washington, found it convenient to accept the interior minister's fingering of Baitullah Mehsud and that ever-useful, all-purpose enemy al-Qaida.

Benazir's murder, Muñoz commented,

> reminds me of the Spanish play *Fuente Ovejuna,* in which the hated ruler of the village Fuente Ovejuna is killed and the magistrate who investigates the crime cannot find the culprit. During the investigation, every villager interrogated declares that Fuente Ovejuna did it. In Benazir's case, it would seem that the village assassinated her: Al-Qaida gave the order; the Pakistani Taliban executed the attack, possibly backed or at least encouraged by members of the Establishment; the Musharraf government facilitated the crime by not providing her with adequate security; local senior policemen attempted a cover-up; Benazir's lead security team failed to properly

safeguard her; and most Pakistani political actors would rather turn the page than continue investigating who was behind the assassination.[4]

Muñoz and his team delivered their somewhat inconclusive report in April 2010. In 2012 — after Musharraf, in exile, had been issued a subpoena for his arrest for failing to provide adequate security to Bhutto, and former police chief Aziz had been charged with criminal conspiracy to murder — interior minister Rehman Malik presented the "final investigation report" by Pakistan's Federal Investigation Agency, which named a staggering twenty-seven terrorist groups as having executed the murder. At the end of that year Pakistan's *Dawn* newspaper described the judicial investigation with resignation: "Repeated and unending investigations, indifferent lawyers, a chaotic judicial system and a government that really didn't care, have all ensured that Benazir Bhutto's trial is going nowhere."[5]

Bhutto had written up a document she called her "political last will and testament" for the members of the PPP on October 16, just before her return to Pakistan. Even she, who had courted danger for so many years, must have been aware that this time there was a strong possibility of assassination. In this document she named as her political heir her son, Bilawal, at that time nineteen years of age. He was to be the future leader of the PPP. Back in 1988 she had denied any dynastic ambitions, responding to *60 Minutes*'s Ed Bradley, who had asked about her newborn son's future, "I don't want him to go into politics. No, no. I think there's been a lot of pain in politics."[6] Even in September 2007, less than three months before her death, she had said she was "very clear that [the children] must not think about politics until they finish their educations and they're older and they're mature; in other words, until they know that's what they want, rather than because their mother's in it." She claimed that she would have liked Bilawal to go into law or medicine.[7] Now she cemented the reputation of the PPP as the Bhutto Family Party by declaring her son — whose name would henceforth be Bilawal Bhutto Zardari — the new chairman, with his father, Asif Ali Zardari, to act as custodial chairman until Bilawal completed his education.

Fatima Bhutto loudly expressed her outrage in the press and, later, in her family history. "This is the legacy Benazir has left behind for Pakistan," she fulminated. "This is the saprophytic culture she created and thrived in. Bloodlines, genetics, a who's who of dynastic politics — this is all her. It is this corrupted and dangerously simple system that allows her husband to rule a country of 180 million people by virtue of having a close enough tie to the dead, to the corpses that demand — and receive — sympathy votes."[8] For yes, by then the inconceivable had actually happened: Asif Ali Zardari, the hated Mr. Ten Percent, had assumed the Bhutto mantle.

In February 2008 the long-delayed elections finally took place. Zardari was the lucky beneficiary of a surge of sympathy from those outraged by his wife's murder. Together, the PPP and the PML (N) under Nawaz Sharif triumphed easily over Musharraf's parliamentary supporters. Zardari and Sharif, old enemies, now agreed to form a coalition government. With the Eighteenth Amendment to the constitution, the country officially returned to parliamentary democracy. Zardari, who declined to serve as prime minister, appointed Yousaf Raza Gillani to that post and then stood in the wings as the Lawyers' Movement, in a concerted blitz of protests and media appeals, finally brought about the military dictator's downfall, bitterly disappointing those in Washington who had hoped Musharraf would continue to share power with the civilian administration. On August 18, with impeachment talk in the air, Musharraf finally resigned the presidency. Three weeks later Zardari — no surprise — was elected to that post. Nawaz Sharif, angry at Zardari's lack of cooperation with his party, withdrew his party from the ruling coalition and repaired to the opposition benches.

Zardari would remain in office until 2013, when Nawaz Sharif reassumed power after his party received a large majority in parliamentary elections. Zardari (or the widower Bhutto, as he is sometimes called), never much loved in his native country, became increasingly unpopular during his years in power. Corruption, inefficiency, and incompetence marked his presidency. Farooq Leghari, Bhutto's president during her second term, appeared on television, claiming that in 1996 Zardari had insisted that Mir Murtaza Bhutto be rubbed out; a few weeks previously, all the policemen accused in Murtaza's assassination had been acquitted in the Karachi Session Court. Mumtaz Ali Bhutto, who had publicly called Zardari a crook, was arrested. The Pakistani press mocked Zardari's primitive superstitions, with *Dawn* accusing him of having black goats sacrificed at the president's house.[9] Eventually the ridicule became so loud that Zardari pushed a "Cyber Crime" bill through the National Assembly, making "spoofing," "satirizing," or "character assassinating" the president a crime punishable by six months to fourteen years in prison.

Bhuttoism is entering a new phase, with Bilawal Bhutto Zardari finally claiming the place in the sun his mother prepared for him. And just what is Bhuttoism, anyway? "For me," Bilawal says, "serving the people . . . is about poverty alleviation."[10] It remains to be seen how sincere he is in this ambition, or how effective he might be at achieving it. He has so far lived a life, if anything, even more removed from Pakistan's common people than his mother or grandfather did, residing in luxury in London and Dubai during his formative years and then attending Oxford, where he gained a reputation as quite a party animal. Although Bilawal, at twenty-seven, has more than achieved his majority, Zardari remains cochairman of the PPP; this dis-

mays many PPP supporters in Pakistan, who urge the son to rid
the party of the tarnished ex-president.

The Benazir Bhutto of 1988 was a uniting figure for her country; that of twenty years later, a divisive one. In retrospect, her
best and her worst qualities seem so intimately linked that the
course of her career might almost have been predicted.

   Her greatest quality was her valor. "I did not believe then
and I do not believe now," Anne Fadiman has said, "that Benazir was a perfect politician. But she had courage of a degree I
had never seen before and never expect to see again."[11] This
is what still makes Bhutto worthy of our attention, makes her
more than just the corrupt, compromised politician her record
in office might indicate. As the Pakistani journalist Bina Shah
wrote in a *New York Times* op-ed piece on the seventh anniver-
sary of Bhutto's death, "Ms. Bhutto left behind more than success or scandal. In her wake are the millions of Pakistani girls
and women who look at her life, her determination, her perse-
verance in the face of all odds . . . They thrill to the idea, still
radical in Pakistan 40 years after Ms. Bhutto began her political career, that gender doesn't have to stop them from achieving
their dreams."[12] The cards might have been stacked in Bhutto's
favor — she was rich, educated, aristocratic, the favored daughter of a very powerful father — nevertheless, her achievement
was a remarkable one. Malala Yousafzai, the Pakistani schoolgirl
and recipient of the 2014 Nobel Peace Prize who survived being
shot in the face in retaliation for her activism on behalf of girls'
education, has cited Bhutto as her personal inspiration. But
then, there is the narcissistic, self-serving Bhutto, addicted, if
not to real power, then to her power over the masses. "I wanted
to like her," photographer Mary Ellen Mark said, speaking of
her days at Bhutto's side during her 1986 triumphal progress,
"but I didn't . . . A diva . . . In a way she was a mind-fucker —

a little like Marlon Brando. Beautiful, powerful, strange. Very driven. Frightening, in a way."[13]

If Bhutto had lost her life in 1988, she would be remembered as a shining example of what youth, fortitude, and idealism can accomplish even in the most brutal and repressive political culture. As it is, her career stands as an object lesson in how great charisma and influence can exacerbate what might in an average life remain a latent character flaw, and inflate it until it subsumes the entire personality. Bhutto's flaw, inherited from and cultivated by her father, was a belief in the special, almost sacred destiny of herself and the Bhutto family: she might well have said, with Shakespeare's Richard II, "Not all the water in the rough rude sea / Can wash the balm from an anointed king."

Bhutto spoke as a democrat, but she thought and felt as a dynast. And the Pakistani voters, who turned out in their millions to vote for the impassioned young woman who promised economic and social reform and an end to poverty and feudal privilege, were disappointed — once again.

Acknowledgments

I could not have written this book without the foundational research done by earlier writers on the Bhutto family. I am particularly indebted to Tariq Ali, Raja Anwar, Shyam Bhatia, and Stanley Wolpert.

I would like to thank Peter Galbraith, Yolanda Kodrzycki, Anne Fadiman, Catherine Drucker, and the late Mary Ellen Mark for discussing their memories of Benazir Bhutto with me.

Endnotes

Introduction

1 William Dalrymple, "Pakistan's Flawed and Feudal Princess," *Observer,* December 29, 2007.
2 Ian Buruma, "The Double Life of Benazir Bhutto," *New York Review of Books,* March 2, 1989.
3 Christopher Hitchens, "Born to Rule: An Exclusive Interview with Benazir Bhutto, Prime Minister of Pakistan," *Vanity Fair,* January 1989.
4 Amy Wilentz, "Benazir Bhutto: The Exile's Return," *More,* December 2007/January 2008.

Chapter 1

1 Stanley Wolpert, *Zulfi Bhutto of Pakistan: His Life and Times* (London and New York: Oxford University Press, 1993), 4.
2 Benazir Bhutto, *Daughter of Destiny: An Autobiography* (New York: Harper Perennial, 2007), 28. *Daughter of Destiny* was first published in Great Britain in 1988 by Hamish Hamilton under the title *Daughter of the East.*
3 Wolpert, *Zulfi Bhutto,* 14.
4 Ibid., 24–5.

Chapter 2

1 Tariq Ali, *The Duel: Pakistan on the Flight Path of American Power* (New York: Scribner, 2008), 43.

2   Ibid., 69.
3   B. Bhutto, *Daughter of Destiny*, 33.
4   James Wynbrandt, *A Brief History of Pakistan* (New York: Checkmark Books, 2009), 196.
5   B. Bhutto, *Daughter of Destiny*, 43.
6   Wilentz, "The Exile's Return."

Chapter 3

1   For a brilliant fictional treatment of families like the Bhuttos and their servants, tenants, and retainers, see Daniyal Mueenuddin's collection of linked short stories, *In Other Rooms, Other Wonders* (New York: W. W. Norton, 2009).
2   Anne Fadiman, "Benazir: Face-to-Face with the Woman Who Wants to Rule Pakistan," *Life*, October 1986.
3   Shyam Bhatia, *Goodbye Shahzadi: A Political Biography of Benazir Bhutto* (New Delhi: Lotus Roli Books, 2008), 3.
4   Anne Fadiman, interview by the author, November 17, 2014.
5   Yolanda Kodrzycki, interview by the author, November 8, 2014.
6   Ibid.
7   Ibid.
8   Anatol Lieven, *Pakistan: A Hard Country* (New York: Public Affairs, 2011), 59.
9   Zulfikar Ali Bhutto, *The Great Tragedy* (Karachi: Pakistan People's Party, 1971).
10 B. Bhutto, *Daughter of Destiny*, 57.
11 Brian Urquhart, *A Life in Peace and War* (New York: Harper & Row, 1987), 204.
12 Ibid., 223.
13 "Secret Affidavit of Yahya Khan," ed. Abu Rushd, *Bangladesh Defense Journal*, February 2009.
14 B. Bhutto, *Daughter of Destiny*, 51–2.
15 Zulfikar Ali Bhutto, Heathrow Airport press conference, December 19, 1971.
16 Henry Kissinger, *White House Years* (Boston: Little, Brown & Co., 1979), 907.

17 Zulfikar Ali Bhutto, *Speeches and Statements,* vol. I (Karachi: Government of Pakistan, 1972), 15–16.

18 Catherine Drucker, interview by the author, October 27, 2014.

19 B. Bhutto, *Daughter of Destiny,* 62.

20 Kodrzycki, interview by the author.

21 Quoted in Kausar Niazi, *Zulfiqar Ali Bhutto: The Last Days* (New Delhi: Vikas, 1992), 99.

22 Tehmina Durrani, *My Feudal Lord* (Lahore: Vanguard Books, 1991), 48.

Chapter 4

1 Bhatia, *Goodbye Shahzadi,* xi.

 2 Hitchens, "Born to Rule."

 3 Bhatia, *Goodbye Shahzadi,* 5.

 4 Ibid., 3

 5 Peter Galbraith, interview by the author, November 1, 2014.

 6 B. Bhutto, *Daughter of Destiny,* 77.

 7 Ibid., 72.

 8 Steven R. Weisman, "The Return of Benazir Bhutto: Struggle in Pakistan," *New York Times,* September 21, 1986.

 9 Drucker, interview by the author.

10 Galbraith, interview by the author.

11 B. Bhutto, *Daughter of Destiny,* 77–8.

12 Wolpert, *Zulfi Bhutto,* 263.

13 Tariq Ali and David Barsamian, *Speaking of Empire and Resistance: Conversations with Tariq Ali* (New York: The New Press, 2005), 143.

14 B. Bhutto, *Daughter of Destiny,* 184.

15 Durrani, *My Feudal Lord,* 109.

Chapter 5

1 B. Bhutto, *Daughter of Destiny,* 95.

 2 Ibid., 102.

 3 Shaikh Aziz, "A Leaf from History: Furious Zia Gets Bhutto Rearrested," *Dawn,* June 18, 2014.

 4 B. Bhutto, *Daughter of Destiny,* 116.

5 Ramsey Clark, "The Trial of Ali Bhutto," *Nation,* August 19–26, 1978.
6 B. Bhutto, *Daughter of Destiny,* 122.
7 Raja Anwar, *The Terrorist Prince: The Life and Death of Murtaza Bhutto* (Lahore: Vanguard Books, 1998), 22.
8 Ibid.
9 B. Bhutto, *Daughter of Destiny,* 126.
10 Ibid., 127–8.
11 This subject is discussed thoroughly in Anatol Lieven's comprehensive study of Pakistani politics and society, *Pakistan: A Hard Country.*
12 Rory McCarthy, "I Never Asked for Power," *Guardian,* August 14, 2002.
13 Ramsey Clark, "The Corruption of Covert Actions," *Covert Action Quarterly,* Fall 1998.
14 Ibid.
15 Ibid.

Chapter 6

1 Husain Haqqani, *Magnificent Delusions: Pakistan, the United States, and an Epic History of Understanding* (New York: Public Affairs, 2013), 242.
2 Something of the climate of the times was captured in the well-known film *Charlie Wilson's War,* which is based on George Crile's book of the same name (New York: Atlantic Monthly Press, 2003), but a more profound account of these shenanigans can be found in Mohammed Hanif's superb satirical novel *A Case of Exploding Mangoes* (New York: Vintage, 2009).
3 Durrani, *My Feudal Lord,* 140–41.
4 Fatima Bhutto, *Songs of Blood and Sword: A Daughter's Memoir* (New York: Nation Books, 2010), 216.
5 Anwar, *The Terrorist Prince,* 58.
6 Galbraith, interview by the author.

Chapter 7

1 *The Reagan Diaries,* ed. Douglas Brinkley (New York: HarperCollins, 2007), 117.
2 Galbraith, interview by the author.
3 Quoted in Bhatia, *Goodbye Shahzadi,* 52.

4 Galbraith, interview by the author.

5 Drucker, interview by the author.

6 B. Bhutto, *Daughter of Destiny,* 267.

7 Ibid., 269.

8 Ibid., 274.

9 F. Bhutto, *Songs of Blood and Sword,* 254.

10 Galbraith, interview by the author.

11 B. Bhutto, *Daughter of Destiny,* 299.

Chapter 8

1 B. Bhutto, *Daughter of Destiny,* 318.

2 Ibid., 322–3.

3 Mary Ellen Mark, interview by the author, October 24, 2014.

4 Ibid.

5 Drucker, interview by the author.

6 Claudia Dreifus, "Real-Life Dynasty: Benazir Bhutto," *New York Times Magazine,* May 15, 1994.

7 Ibid.

8 Howell Raines, "Benazir Bhutto to Marry, in a Pact by 2 Families," *New York Times,* July 31, 1987.

9 Christina Lamb, "My Life with Benazir," *Times Online,* December 30, 2007.

10 Raines, "Bhutto to Marry."

11 Lamb, "My Life with Benazir."

12 Stephanie Salmon, "10 Things You Didn't Know About Benazir Bhutto," *U.S. News and World Report,* December 27, 2007.

13 Anne Fadiman, "Behind the Veil," *Life,* February 1988.

14 Ibid.

15 Ibid.

16 Kodrzycki, interview by the author.

17 Durrani, *My Feudal Lord,* 77.

Chapter 9

1 Edward Jay Epstein, "Who Killed Zia?," *Vanity Fair,* September 1989.

2 Barbara Crossette, "Who Killed Zia?," *World Policy Journal,* Fall 2005.

3 Hitchens, "Born to Rule."
4 Kamila Shamsie, "Pop Idols," *Granta* 112 (August 2010).
5 Lawrence Wright, "The Double Game," *The New Yorker,* May 16, 2011.
6 B. Bhutto, *Daughter of Destiny,* 379.
7 "The Prime Minister," *60 Minutes,* aired March 5, 1989.
8 Galbraith, interview by the author.
9 Ibid.
10 Haqqani, *Magnificent Delusions,* 278.

Chapter 10

1 B. Bhutto, *Daughter of Destiny,* 392.
2 Benazir Bhutto, interview by Robert MacNeil, *MacNeil/Lehrer News-Hour,* PBS, December 16, 1988.
3 Ibid.
4 Bhatia, *Goodbye Shahzadi,* 93.
5 See Wynbrandt, *History of Pakistan,* 239.
6 "The Prime Minister," *60 Minutes,* aired March 5, 1989.
7 Drucker, interview by the author.
8 Ali and Barsamian, *Speaking of Empire,* 115.
9 F. Bhutto, *Songs of Blood and Sword,* 289.
10 Fadiman, interview by the author.
11 Seymour Hersh, "Defending the Arsenal," *The New Yorker,* November 16, 2009.
12 Seymour Hersh, "On the Nuclear Edge," *The New Yorker,* March 29, 1993.

Chapter 11

1 Shamsie, "Pop Idols."
2 F. Bhutto, *Songs of Blood and Sword,* 303.
3 Barbara Crossette, "Bhutto Is Dismissed in Pakistan After 20 Months," *New York Times,* August 7, 1990.
4 Molly Moore, "Bhutto Elected Pakistan's Premier, Says She Hopes to End Isolation," *Washington Post,* October 20, 1993.
5 Bhatia, *Goodbye Shahzadi,* 39.
6 Ibid., 43.

7   Riaz Haq, "Musharraf Earned Legitimacy by Good Governance," *Haq's Musings* (blog), September 27, 2010, http://www.riazhaq.com/2014/01/musharraf-earned-legitimacy-by-good.html.

8   Wynbrandt, *History of Pakistan,* 255.

9   John F. Burns, "House of Graft: Chasing the Bhutto Millions," *New York Times,* January 9, 1998.

10 Ibid.

11 Ibid.

12 Dalrymple, "Pakistan's Flawed and Feudal Princess."

13 All of this turned up in an investigation by Transparency International on behalf of the Pakistani government.

Chapter 12

1   Anwar, *The Terrorist Prince,* 201.

2   Henry Kamm, "Karachi Journal: With Blood Tie Sundered, Blood Divides Bhuttos," *New York Times,* January 12, 1994.

3   Michael Fathers, "The Battle of All Mothers," *Independent,* December 14, 1993.

4   Henry Kamm, "Bhutto Fans the Family Feud, Charging Mother Favors Son," *New York Times,* January 14, 1994.

5   Dreifus, "Real-Life Dynasty."

6   All these citations are from the Amnesty International report *Pakistan: The Pattern Persists,* January 1995.

7   F. Bhutto, *Songs of Blood and Sword,* 403.

8   Ali, *The Duel,* 175.

9   Owen Bennett-Jones, "Questions Concerning the Murder of Benazir Bhutto," *London Review of Books,* December 6, 2012.

Chapter 13

1   Benazir Bhutto, "Punishment — Make It Swift, Severe," *Los Angeles Times,* May 17, 1998.

2   Emily MacFarquhar, "Benazir and the Bomb," Alicia Patterson Foundation, Washington, DC, 1998.

3   John Bingham, "Asif Ali Zardari: Life and Style of Pakistan's Mr 10 Per Cent," *Telegraph,* August 3, 2010.

4 Sebastian O'Kelly, "Inside Benazir Bhutto's Looted Palace," *Mail Online,* July 27, 2010.
5 "Benazir Bhutto: The Investigation," BBC, October 30, 2007.
6 Burns, "House of Graft."
7 Ibid.
8 Owen Bennett-Jones, *Pakistan: Eye of the Storm* (New Haven, CT: Yale University Press, 2009), 235.
9 Wilentz, "The Exile's Return."
10 Ibid.
11 McCarthy, "I Never Asked for Power."
12 Ibid.

Chapter 14

1 Adrian Levy and Cathy Scott-Clark, "The Plot to Bring Back Benazir," *Guardian,* July 20, 2007.
2 Ali, *The Duel,* 160.
3 Ibid.
4 Isambard Wilkinson, "Benazir Bhutto Sets Price of Musharraf Deal," *Telegraph,* July 30, 2007.
5 Fatima Bhutto, "Aunt Benazir's False Promises," *Los Angeles Times,* November 14, 2007.
6 Heraldo Muñoz, *Getting Away with Murder: Benazir Bhutto's Assassination and the Politics of Pakistan* (New York: W. W. Norton & Co., 2013), 147.
7 B. Bhutto, *Daughter of Destiny,* 432.
8 Isambard Wilkinson, "Benazir Bhutto's Triumphal Return to Pakistan," *Telegraph,* October 18, 2007.
9 "Pakistan Frees Bhutto, Installs Caretaker Premier," NPR, November 16, 2007.
10 Isambard Wilkinson, "Nawaz Sharif Returns to Pakistan," *Telegraph,* November 26, 2007.

Chapter 15

1 Bennett-Jones, "Questions Concerning the Murder of Benazir Bhutto."
2 Muñoz, *Getting Away with Murder,* 161.

3   Ibid., 158.

4   Ibid., 184–5.

5   Ibid., 202–3.

6   B. Bhutto, interview by Ed Bradley.

7   Wilentz, "The Exile's Return."

8   F. Bhutto, *Songs of Blood and Sword,* 433.

9   "Goats Sacrificed 'to Ward Off Evil Eyes,'" *Dawn,* January 27, 2010.

10 Mehreen Zahra-Malik, "Scion of Pakistan's Bhutto Dynasty Throws Down Gauntlet to PM," Reuters, October 23, 2014.

11 Fadiman, interview by the author.

12 Bina Shah, "The Legacy of Benazir Bhutto," *New York Times,* December 26, 2014.

13 Mark, interview by the author.